1994

DANCING WITH THE PEN
The Learner as a Writer

*Dancing in all its forms cannot be excluded from the curriculum of all noble education:
dancing with the feet, with ideas, with words, and need I add that one must also be able to
dance with the pen?*

Frederich Nietzsche, *The Twilight of the Gods*

Dancing with the Pen

The Learner as a Writer

Ministry of Education

Learning Media
Wellington

Published for the Ministry of Education by
Learning Media Ltd, Box 3293, Wellington, New Zealand.

Third impression 1994

Distributed in the United States of America by
Richard C. Owen Publishers Inc., Box 585, Katonah, NY 10536.
Distributed in Australia by
Troll Books of Australia, Box 522, Roseville, New South Wales 2069.

Dewey number 372.6
ISBN 0 478 05560 9
Item number 92/213

Contents

New Zealand Teachers' Beliefs About Literacy Learning and Teaching

- Reading and writing experiences should be "child centred".
- Reading and writing for meaning are paramount.
- Writing should have purpose and meaning.
- Literacy learning must always be rewarding.
- Reading and writing are inseparable processes.
- Children learn to read and write by reading and writing many different kinds of texts.
- Reading and writing are powerful tools for learning.
- Reading and writing fulfil a variety of functions.
- The best approach to teaching reading and writing is a combination of approaches.
- Good first teaching is essential for continuing success in reading and writing.
- The foundations of literacy are laid at home in the early years.
- Reading and writing flourish in a supportive community.
- Success at reading and writing encourages further reading and writing.

Introduction

This book for primary teachers aims to develop their understanding of how children learn to write and how teachers can facilitate the process. The authors have focused on the learner's role, and have stressed the importance of responding to what the learner-writer is trying to do.

Much of what has been written in this book has been built on the practice of teachers, and greatly influenced by the work of several outstanding New Zealand educators, particularly Sylvia Ashton Warner, Elwyn Richardson, Don Holdaway, and Marie Clay. Their work has helped New Zealand teachers in developing their understanding of the teaching of reading and writing.

Rather than being concerned only with the product, teachers today pay more attention to the processes children are engaged in as they write, and the learning which occurs when children are in control of their writing. Teachers' focus is on helping writers become aware of how and why they write, and on encouraging them to write freely, fluently, and well. Teachers see how being aware of the writing process helps students use writing as a tool for learning. But not only that, for the emphasis on the process does not mean that the product is unimportant—the aim of writing is always to produce something that can be read.[1]

In the past, many teachers did not view writing as a complex developmental process. They were more concerned with the finished product, which they evaluated without regard to the way it was produced. Teachers seldom looked beyond surface features—the weaknesses of spelling, punctuation, grammar, and usage. Some, instead of offering just enough help when it was needed, took control away from beginning writers and said, "Tell me your story, and I'll write it for you." So some writers learned only to trace over, or copy under. Writing was seldom considered as a tool for communicating, recording, and understanding.

In the early 1980s, following the visit of Donald Graves to New Zealand, teachers took up the idea of "process writing" with enthusiasm. However, the workshop organisation of teaching writing suggested by Graves, in which time was set aside for an intensive writing session each day, was given more emphasis than his underlying philosophy. Teachers encouraged students' process writing with vigour, but many found that the results were not satisfactory. It seemed that students were now writing freely, but not producing

7

good quality writing, or gaining greater skills in writing across the curriculum. Nor were their skills in writing linked to their developing skills in reading. The root cause was a lack of understanding on the part of teachers of the writing process itself.

New Zealand teachers had long been aware of the need to make reading a child-centred and meaningful experience in which the role of the learner was of critical importance. Now came the realisation that the writing process is not a method of organisation, a teaching approach, or something done for six weeks and then put aside. Nor is it something children do for thirty minutes a day only in a writing workshop. Writing, like reading, concerns the development of the child as a communicator of thoughts and feelings in all areas of the curriculum and for a variety of reasons.

This book recognises the close links between reading and writing. As Marie Clay says, "For children who learn to write at the same time as they learn to read, writing plays a significant part in the early reading process."[2] In recognising the close relationships between writing and reading, this book builds on New Zealand teachers' understandings of how children learn to read, and explores and explains recent thinking on the writing process.

The writing examples in the book range across the whole primary school. This is because the aspects of writing described affect all writers in largely the same way although, in their application, learners may make use of different content, and teachers different approaches. While the book gives much practical advice on teaching approaches, it does not spell out detailed methodology, nor does it examine in detail the development of the writer at the emergent, early, and fluency stages. The general aspects described in this book will be supported by future resources which relate to both reading and writing development at all levels. However, a short description of the very young learner-writer, and writing for new learners of English, is included in Appendix 2.

In summary, this book is designed to assist teachers by:
- **bringing them to a fuller understanding of the writing process;**
- **helping them create a teaching environment in which learners feel confident to develop their writing;**
- **helping them understand how children learn to write;**
- **providing them with some ways to foster writing development.**

1

Beliefs and Principles

The power of words

When A. S. Byatt was a child, she visited her grandfather's boiled sweet factory. She saw there a huge shed, filled with vats of boiling sugar.

> *I wrote about this [at school]. It is the first piece of writing I remember clearly as mine, the first time I remember choosing words, fixing something. I remember, still, two words I chose. Both were from my reading. One was . . . "spun-glass". The word had always delighted me, with its contradiction between the brittle and the flexible thread produced. I remember I used it for the fragments [of sugar] in our conical paper bags. I remember also casting about for a way of telling how violent, how powerful were the colours in the sugar vats. I wrote that the green was "emerald" and I know where I found that word, in the reading endlessly supplied by my mother. "And ice, mast-high, came floating by / As green as emerald." As green as emerald. Did I go on to other jewels? I don't remember. But I do remember that I took the pleasure in writing my account of the boiling sugar that I usually took only in reading. Words were there to be used.* [3]

Words empower us. They enable us to define reality, or create it. In retelling our experiences or listening to others, in writing experience down or reading others' words, we enlarge our lives, cross frontiers of knowledge.

The first and most important use of language is to communicate with others, but it is much more than this. Trying to express what we really mean involves the active exploration of ideas. This process involves us in reflective thought and in the selection and arrangement of appropriate language. The practice gained through this experience becomes part of the thinking tools used in subsequent productions—as Gordon Wells says, "harnessing the dynamo of language" to power our own thinking.[4]

We write for many purposes but usually to record events and ideas, to share with others or to reflect on later. This gives what we write purpose and meaning.

Writing has a variety of forms, which depend on the purpose for the writing.

Writing takes many forms. Our particular purpose for writing and our intended audience influence the way we present each message and convey our meaning. As experience with a variety of examples and models grows, we become more flexible in choosing the most appropriate form of saying something, and more skilful in reaching our intended audience. Our range of linguistic options increases.

Oral and written language

Although this book is about writing, talk is central to learning. It provides the foundation on which we learn to read and write.

There are always parallels between oral and written forms, but also important differences. Everyday talk is informal—hesitant, repetitive, often relying on non-verbal language to make meaning clear. Listeners can ask questions, and speakers can clarify confusions. Writing for an audience has to be more careful, more reflective. Published words do not offer us second chances. They require precision for ourselves as well as for the reader.

Reading and writing, like talking and listening, are inseparable processes.

Talking and listening are two sides of the act of communication. Reading and writing are as closely linked. Readers use their own knowledge and experience to construct meaning **from** text; writers to construct meaning **in** text. To communicate successfully, children need to read like writers and write like readers. They can then see the elements common to both forms of expression—that both are purposeful, express meaning, share the same functions, and use the same print conventions.

Because writers need to read in order to create and re-create meanings, and to construct and organise thoughts and ideas, reading is an integral part of the writing process. During writing, writers use many kinds of language knowledge in constructing texts, and in organising their thoughts and ideas. In particular, they re-read their scripts to match what has been written with what is intended. Reading, therefore, goes hand in hand with writing. Teachers should make this link clear. Don Holdaway comments:

> *Instruction has persistently separated reading from writing in a way that would be insufferable in learning to listen and talk. The two modes form an integral nexus of learning around common processes, and this, too, may be readily reflected in teaching. There are no logical or practical excuses for the dismemberment of literacy—only instructional precedents.*[5]

Child-centred learning

Writing can give voice to personal meaning. It is one of the ways in which we explore our meaning of our world. It enables us to discover, clarify, and share personal interpretations of events and ideas.

From an early age, children can express their ideas of the world around them through movement, talk, drawing, and writing. They do this with vitality and confidence. When their ideas are acknowledged by a supportive audience, in a trusted learning community, the learner gains confidence in expressing further personal discoveries. Children's learning should be of the kind in which, predominantly, they make their own decisions about what to say and how to go about saying it. They will then see the value of their writing in learning and communicating about their world.

Writing contributes to the growth and realisation of self.

Writing experiences should be child centred.

Literacy learning must always be rewarded.

Responsibility and independence

When children are encouraged to make their own decisions about learning tasks, what they write is not fragmented. This is because their decisions are about what *they* see as integral to their meaning. Many will need advice on clarifying what they are writing, but being able to make decisions themselves shows that they are gaining control of their own learning.

Teachers need to have faith in children's learning ability.

Culture and literacy

What a particular cultural group sees as an important use of literacy has a dominant influence on what children believe, and the ease with which they learn. By knowing and accepting the writer's background, teachers can adapt their own ways of teaching to accommodate the needs of children.

Children have learned a tremendous amount about their world by the time they start school, but their world and the world of school may seem radically different. At home, there is the shared memory of common experiences which often goes hand in hand with learning new skills and making sense of new ideas. Barbara Tizard and Martin Hughes point out that, in talking things over at home, parents and caregivers make use of a hundred private analogies and explanations which a teacher cannot hope to share.[6] Asking questions, listening to adult talk, or watching grown-ups may be a natural way children have enlarged their understandings. In the inevitably

The teaching of writing should accommodate children's diverse cultural backgrounds.

less personal context of school, teachers can help children add to their store of knowledge by trying to make use of familiar ways of learning as well as introducing new ones.

Patterns of talking and listening, reading and writing differ from one cultural group to another.[7] For some children from a largely oral background, there is a special need to see their culture given the status of written as well as oral expression—to see it, as Patricia Grace says, "legitimised in literature". [8]

The best approach to teaching reading and writing is a combination of approaches.

Teachers who use patterns appropriate to the cultures children come from reinforce a child's sense of identity in the new and strange environment of school. For each teacher, the important thing is to listen to the signals that children give as they work towards communication, and build on the competencies they already have.

A literacy environment is not separable from the social fabric . . . of the family. [9]

Expectation

Learners' writings reflect their own expectations and the expectations of those around them.

Learners are powerfully influenced by the expectations of peers and adults around them. Those who expect to succeed are most likely to succeed. Learners need to *know* they will learn to read and write successfully. Teachers should convey the strong expectation that children will learn to write successfully. It should be as obvious and natural as parents' belief that their children will learn to speak. Children will develop as writers when they work in an environment which assumes they will succeed—this is most important. Teachers must convey the expectation that writing will reach a high standard and can be shared successfully with others. **The expectation that children will write and the value placed on their writing are key conditions in influencing children's attitudes towards writing.**

Patricia Grace says:

> *I've always enjoyed writing, but I didn't know that being a writer was something I could aspire to—it didn't occur to me that I could be a writer. I thought that writers had to have travelled, or swum Cook Strait, or climbed mountains, or had a terrible childhood.* [10]

Value, praise, and success

If children are to develop as writers, they need to experiment and take risks in their writing and learn from the consequences of their choices. They will do this in a classroom where the teacher values their contributions and efforts.

When writers experience the challenge and sense of achievement associated with successful writing, they feel encouraged to continue to write for a variety of purposes, both in and outside the classroom. Being a successful writer enhances learning and increases self-esteem. In turn, this increased confidence fosters independence, enquiry, risk-taking, and personal growth.

Success at writing encourages further writing.

Those children who come from communities which place different values on oral and written language may need special effort and encouragement from the teacher to re-create their spoken language

Good first teaching is essential for continuing success in writing.

in writing. Some others may bring experience of reading and writing which does not match what is asked of them in school. But, whatever their backgrounds, children must feel that their efforts are valued and their progress acknowledged. Praise is a wonderful spur to achievement. No matter how immature children's attempts at written forms, teachers need to respond first with warmth to what is being said, and then offer sufficient sympathetic guidance to make a *real* difference in the quality of the message.

Honesty in writing must be valued.

Teachers must value children's own experience and help them to be true to it in honest writing. Patricia Grace's comments emphasise the need to respect each child's integrity in writing:

> *One time we were asked to write from our own experience, and it was quite difficult to feel you had an experience worthy of writing about. When the teacher came back with that piece of writing, she said, "Did you really see primroses?" And I said, "Oh no, but I saw some flowers, and I called them primroses." And I think it was then that the penny dropped that, when you're writing from your own experience, everything has to ring true to that experience .[11]*

Response and the importance of listening

Writers need a supportive response.

Learner writers need to talk to others about their work. Others need to listen and respond. Response is another important condition necessary for writing to flourish.

Lucy Calkins points out that teachers often *appear* to listen to a learner's work, but instead of giving a natural reaction, such as laughing, sighing, smiling, or reflecting, they tend to look for questions in an effort to "improve" the writing.[12] Sometimes a teacher may even suggest changing the message in the learner's writing to conform to their own experiences and social norms. They take over the ownership of the writing, and the result may be a work more technically correct, but one that no longer means anything to the writer. They have not been acknowledged in the discussion. The "conference" has really been a monologue because the teacher has not realised that the first purpose in writing is to express and share meaning.

Writing for meaning is paramount.

The writer's message and their voice must always be a valued starting point. Although "getting it right" may be important, it is not the reason why writers write and share their writing. Teachers need

Butterflies
by Patricia Grace

The grandmother plaited her granddaughter's hair and then she said, "Get your lunch. Put it in your bag. Get your apple. You come straight back after school, straight home here. Listen to the teacher," she said. "Do what she say."

Her grandfather was out on the step. He walked down the path with her and out on to the footpath. He said to a neighbour, "Our granddaughter goes to school. She lives with us now."

"She's fine," the neighbour said. "She's terrific with her two plaits in her hair."

"And clever," the grandfather said. "Writes every day in her book."

"She's fine," the neighbour said.

The grandfather waited with his granddaughter by the crossing and then he said, "Go to school. Listen to the teacher. Do what she say."

When the granddaughter came home from school her grandfather was hoeing around the cabbages. Her grandmother was picking beans. They stopped their work.

"You bring your book home?" the grandmother asked.

"Yes."

"You write your story?"

"Yes."

"What's your story?"

"About the butterflies."

"Get your book, then. Read your story."

The grandmother took her book from her schoolbag and opened it.

"I killed all the butterflies," she read. "This is me and this is all the butterflies."

"And your teacher like your story, did she?"

"I don't know."

"What your teacher say?"

"She said butterflies are beautiful creatures. They hatch out and fly in the sun. The butterflies visit all the pretty flowers, she said. They lay their eggs and then they die. You don't kill butterflies, that's what she said."

The grandmother and grandfather were quiet for a long time, and their granddaughter, holding the book, stood quite still in the warm garden.

"Because you see," the grandfather said, "your teacher she buys all her cabbages from the supermarket and that's why."

Teachers need to teach the writer and not the writing.

As well as valuing current work, teachers need to signpost ways to proceed.

The foundations of literacy are laid at home in the early years.

to teach the writer and not the writing through methods centred on them and their message.

Learners are encouraged and supported when those around them respond with interest and sensitivity, and with constructive guidance. As well as valuing what the learner has currently done, teachers need to hone skills, extend knowledge, and signpost ways to proceed. They can do this by talking to learners about their writing as individuals as well as in group and class sharing sessions.

Environment

The home environment of children is a powerful force on their success in writing. Children who have been encouraged to express or reflect on their feelings, ideas, and experiences, and to talk these through, delight in language. They quickly understand the power that purposeful control of language gives.

Children who see their parents and caregivers read and write with pleasure and as a matter of course, who are surrounded by books and writing of all kinds, whose attention is drawn to the words that surround all of us in our everyday lives—useful words, funny words, informative words, exciting words—are emerging as readers and writers long before they come to school. They will have scribbled, painted, and made their marks on paper, as they have seen others do.

For those who have not experienced this love affair with written words, it is the teacher's responsibility to provide a classroom setting that encourages children to write, and to give them help when needed. Children at school should have the same daily opportunities to write as they have to speak and read—about all manner of things in and outside the classroom.

A stimulating and comfortable environment, both in the classroom and the school, where the children are surrounded by printed material in the form of books, posters, notices, charts, and attractive displays of their own work also helps to create a *purpose* for writing. Children should know that what they write in school is as useful, important, and valuable as the writing that goes on outside.

Conditions that promote writing depend on more than physical surroundings. Learners need to be part of a community of writers who trust and support each other, and who respect each other's thoughts and ideas. In this community, the teacher is also a trusted writer.

Writing flourishes in a supportive community.

As part of a writing community, their school work should be treated in the same way as that of writers in the world outside school. These writers may be known authors, but are more likely to be

people in their own family or community, writing to fulfil real needs, such as writing notes to the milk vendor, leaving messages for the family, keeping a society's minutes book, or sending news to distant family members. Teachers should be aware that some children may be writing for more varied purposes at home than they do at school. A close contact with parents, who in many ways act as first teachers, often reveals a richness of writing experience rather than a dearth.

The social environment of the classroom, therefore, is as important as the physical environment. In every class, the diversity of background and experiences enriches what children can learn from each other. Children should be encouraged both to share their ideas and talk about their writing, and also respond to and respect the ideas of others.

Immersion in models and demonstrations

Writers need to be immersed in written language.

We cannot all re-invent the wheel. We learn from the examples of others. The richness of the examples which surround successful learners are of vital importance. They need to be in constant contact with a wide variety of meaningful language, both spoken and written—they need to be immersed in written language just as they were immersed in talk when they were learning to speak.

Learners need demonstrations of how writing works.

Learners need demonstrations of how proficient writers work through aspects of the writing process, and the decisions they make while writing. They need models of the written product read aloud to them, or provided in shared book experiences, guided, or independent reading. They need to discuss how the effects in these texts are created.

Teachers need to relate these demonstrations and models, where possible, to an example from home. When a learning experience is put into this kind of context, a child may think, "Oh, is *that* all it is! I know how to do that!" and apply the skills learnt at home to the work at school.

Children learn to write by reading and writing many different kinds of texts.

In such conditions, children find out what other writers have to say, and how they say it. They expand the repertoire of information and strategies which they can use in their own writing, and are introduced to all genres of writing and the forms each takes. This enables them to experiment with different forms, writing styles, and language structures. It increases their control over writing for a particular purpose.

18

Practice and use

Writing is a craft—it can be taught and learnt. By exploring and gaining control over new ways in which to present ideas, learners give effective expression to their imagination and many of their needs, for once a craft is learnt, the skill can be used for many purposes—all different but all creative.

Sylvia Cassedy says:

. . . any writing, fact or fiction, is creative if it reflects the personal perceptions or thinking of the author and is expressed in his or her own words. Your report on frogs or zeppelins can be creative if the planning, organisation, and writing are your very own. [13]

Skill and high quality depend on experience and practice—becoming skilled in a craft takes time. An essential condition is the time and opportunity for learners to practise. Then they will have the chance to gain control over what they are learning and put it to other uses. Writing is not an end in itself—it is a means to many ends.

Writing is creative—a craft that can be taught and learnt.

Learners must have time to practise what they are learning.

Approximations

Learners work confidently, and are more prepared to "have a go", when they know that teachers will accept and encourage their approximations. When this condition holds, they learn through making attempts, even if some of these are not completely successful. This parallels their experience in learning to talk and in learning to read. With their teacher's help, they increase their writing skills, and come nearer to excellence. Growing skill is matched with a growing sense of self-confidence in which learners are able to make choices, take risks, and challenge their own thinking.

Engagement

However well organised the learning environment, learning will not take place unless writers make something of it for themselves. Brian Cambourne insists that while "immersion and demonstration are **necessary** conditions for learning to occur, they are not in themselves **sufficient**. . . . The missing factor is what Frank Smith calls 'engagement'."[14] Frank Smith explains this term in these words:

I use the term "engagement" advisedly for the productive interaction of a brain with a demonstration, because the image I have is of meshing of gears. Learning occurs when the learner engages with a demonstration, so that it, in effect, becomes the learner's demonstration. . . . Engagement takes place in the presence of appropriate demonstrations whenever we are sensitive to learning, and sensitivity is an absence of expectation that learning will not take place. Sensitivity does not need to be accounted for; its absence does.[15]

Engagement with written experience must take place before children can become writers.

For engagement to take place, then, it is essential that children are **actively** involved in immersion and demonstration. They need to **take part in** these experiences and perceive them as ones they can own and re-create themselves. They must see a worthwhile reason to **appropriate what they have seen or heard and expect to make use of it for their own purposes.** Unless these conditions are fulfilled, teaching may simply "wash over them and be ignored."[16]

Engagement is more than involvement: it implies creative interaction with experience. [17]

Helping children grow as writers

To encourage children's writing development, therefore, teachers need to:

- **know how children learn;**
- **know how to facilitate learning through children's awareness of their own language skills;**
- **enable children to believe that writing involves exploring a subject, gathering and linking ideas, noticing new things, and making discoveries which solve problems;**
- **realise that writing is a process of discovery about the world and about self, and a confidence and willingness to communicate that discovery to others.**

2

The Writing Process

Why do we write?

Writing is one of the ways in which we explore our understanding of the world and discover the meaning of our experiences. Writing contributes in its own special way to the growth and realisation of self, and enables us to discover, make clear, and share personal interpretations of events and ideas. We therefore write *for a purpose.*

Donald Murray says that writing is the act of using "language to discover meaning in experience and communicate it."[18] This definition covers a multitude of language functions—some less striking but no less useful than others. Below are listed, together with the forms in which they often appear, some of the many purposes we use writing for in our daily lives—to coax or influence others, to communicate joys or sorrows, to rage, to delight, to praise, to comment, criticise, remind—to do a multitude of things.

To record events	lists, diaries, commentaries, autobiographies, letters, research notes, minutes of meetings, letters or notes to family or friends, transcriptions, reports, family history (whakapapa/genealogies)
To explain	charts, recipes, brochures, captions, instructions, character sketches, definitions, excuses, game rules, handbooks, textbooks
To hypothesise	theories, arguments, proofs
To persuade	job applications, instructions, graffiti, advertisements, arguments, invitations, signs, placards, warnings, record covers, submissions
To invite a response	questions, complaints, invitations, lost and found notices, notes, requests, wanted notices

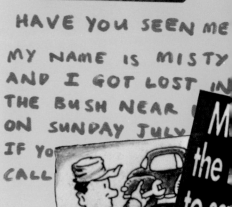

To predict	horoscopes, forecasts, timetables, graphs
To command, direct, or request	directions, invitations, letters, instructions, protests, rules, lists, requisitions, warnings
To amuse, entertain	quizzes, bumper stickers, graffiti, rumours
To narrate	fables, film strips, bedtime stories, myths, sub-titles, superstitions
To invent	plays, anecdotes, jokes, riddles, exaggerations, commercials, puzzles, poems, nursery rhymes, lyrics, slogans
To inform	grooming tips, announcements, book jackets, certificates, labels, news broadcasts, instructions, menus, posters, reports, lists, pamphlets, surveys, timetables, brochures, catalogues, reviews, weather forecasts, graphs, pamphlets
To find out	interviews, questionnaires, surveys, observations
To invite reflection	questions, quizzes, quotations
To summarise	synopses, postcards, reports, verdicts, signs
To comment or give an opinion	editorials, viewpoints, placards

The use of writing in all these forms is one of our creative ways of interacting with our world. It follows that the writing we develop in school, *no matter in what aspect of the curriculum,* is creative writing.

How do we write?

Writing is a craft. This means that it can be learnt, and its skills developed to a high degree through informed practice. Studies of what writers do when they write have identified certain processes common to most writing occasions.

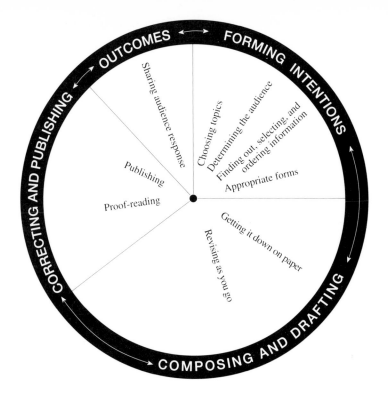

A Model of the Writing Process

This model does not imply that a piece of writing is completed in one turn of the circle. The process is not one of sorting out ideas, getting words down, and then tidying them up—its nature is recursive, that is, the writer's movement from one stage to another is affected by what has gone before and what is anticipated: outcomes may influence the choice of a new topic; the completeness of the information gathered and the skill with which it is organised will affect drafting and revision; drafting may throw up the need for more information, causing the writer to retrace steps to a previous stage; even at the proof-reading stage, making a correction may lead the writer back beyond revision to gathering and organising more information; an alteration at any one stage may have a ripple effect far downstream. The stages in the writing process are therefore not discrete. They influence, and are influenced by, each other.

It is important, too, to remember that not all pieces of writing are developed to the point of sharing with a wider audience.

Forming intentions

During this stage,[19] the writer clarifies the purpose for writing, gathers information, and tests ideas about content and form in relation to the audience proposed. Forming intentions for writing can involve the writer in thinking, talking, drawing, remembering, reflecting, searching for more information, and organising all this into rough sections or sequences. This may take place before, during, and after the actual drafting. These behaviours can be clearly identified, and are described in chapter 3, "The Writing Process in Action".

Composing and drafting

Writing is the easily observable process of translating thoughts, ideas, and intentions into a form of graphic representation. This process is often typified by bursts of seemingly automatic writing as ideas seek expression in the form of words, phrases, and sentences. The writing of immature writers at this stage can be slow and halting as they cope with developing handwriting skills and concentrate on the conventions of spelling.

As writers' intentions become represented on paper, they frequently reread the text to establish how their work is developing with regard to the original plan. Departures from the original plan may be made and, during this stage of writing and revising, writers may attend to details such as correcting spelling, punctuation, or grammar. However, concern with changes to surface features at this stage may hinder the composing process, as attention is diverted from the meaning of the writing.

Revision arises from a need to modify a text to more clearly represent an intended meaning. It enables the writer to further plan and draft. The writer has both control of the writing, and also opportunity to re-organise the original plan so that the writing can now follow previously unthought-of directions. The focus here is on clarifying and shaping meaning, and can involve changes to content and structure. The writing on the page is something to reshape, recraft, remould, until the intention becomes clear.

Correcting and publishing[20]

Once the general shape of a text is fixed, it remains to ensure that the writer's intentions are made clear to the intended audience. Correcting and proof-reading are the preparation of an accurate

24

text for a readership beyond the writer. Modifications to the surface features of spelling, punctuation, grammar, and concern for neatness have not dominated the writing so far because the emphasis has been on meaning. It is important that these surface features or conventions are used accurately to help readers get the intended message. Writers who respect readers will proof-read and correct their writing as far as they can. The teacher can then help with final details about which the writer is still unsure.

A text treated in this way is now ready to be shared with others. An essential outcome of proof-reading is a text that others can read easily. Publication and sharing make the labour of correcting and proof-reading worthwhile.

Outcomes

Through publishing, sharing, and reflecting on their own work, writers find out whether they have fulfilled their intentions for writing. The outcomes of publishing and sharing provide writers with responses from their readers. A warm response, praise, and encouragement enhance the writer's confidence. Success enables success. From a position of confidence, the writer is better able to accept justifiable criticism. Equally important is the personal response writers obtain by reflecting on their own writing. All such responses help writers to discover how effective or valuable their writing has been. They also confirm what the writers have learnt about how to write, and their new insights into the world around them. From here, they can see the path ahead.

151,866

3

The Writing Process in Action

> ### The Thin Prison
> *Hold the pen close to your ear.*
> *Listen—can you hear them?*
> *Words burning as a flame,*
> *Words glittering like a tear,*
>
> *Locked, all locked in the slim pen.*
> *They are crying out for freedom.*
> *And you can release them,*
> *Set them running from prison.*
>
> *Himalayas, balloons, Captain Cook,*
> *Kites, red bricks, London Town,*
> *Sequins, cricket bats, large brown*
> *Boots, lions and lemonade—look,*
>
> *I've just let them out!*
> *Pick up your pen, and start,*
> *Think of the things you know—then*
> *Let the words dance from your pen.*

Leslie Norris [21]

This chapter considers the four main aspects of the writing process described in chapter 2, and their implications for learners and teachers at all levels of the primary school. The examples range across the primary school, but particular emphases are noted under "the teacher's role".

Each aspect is divided into sections which deal with :

- **key learning outcomes** of that aspect of the process;
- **the learner's role,** containing an expansion of these outcomes, and giving an overview of the learner's understandings and behaviours;
- **the teacher's role**;
- **learning through writing** in the particular aspect of the process.

Teachers may use the understandings and behaviours listed in the overview statements to monitor their students' writing development as well as their own teaching strategies.

The key learning outcomes are supported by the ideas in the section on the teacher's role, and by the criteria in the table (page 121) describing writers' characteristics at the emergent, early, and fluency stages.

Significant examples of the learner's understandings and behaviours are demonstrated through photographs of students at work and examples of their writing.

Forming Intentions

Choosing Topics

Learners write best on topics they own. This does not always mean that they have selected their topics without help or stimulus. It does mean that they will have something to say in their own voice about their subject and, therefore, the best purpose of all for writing.

> *A writer needs three things, experience, observation, and imagination, any two of which, at times any one of which, can supply the lack of the others.*

> William Faulkner in *Writers at Work : First Series*

Key learning outcomes

In choosing topics successfully, learners will:

- value first-hand experience and their own knowledge;
- make use of their surroundings, both inside and outside school;
- discuss their ideas freely;
- research their ideas in a variety of ways;
- adapt and make use of their own and others' material and suggestions;
- show initiative in selecting their own topics for writing;
- feel confident enough to muse on selecting a topic.

The learner's role

Learners ask, "What am I going to write about?"

Own knowledge

I can draw a picture about something I know, and write about it. I can write about what I already know—what I think and feel are important. I can keep and refer to my personal topic list.

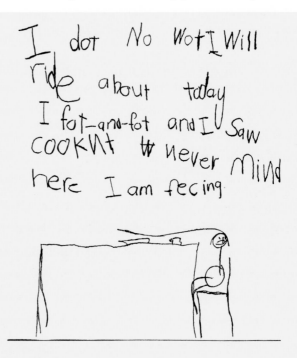

I don't know what I will write about today.
I thought and thought and I still couldn't, never mind.
Here I am thinking.

Surroundings

I can write about many things that are going on in the classroom and outside. I can find things to write about from:
    what I have seen, what I've talked about,
    what I have heard, what I have read.

Discussion

I can explore my own ideas for a topic by talking:
    with the teacher,
    with other people,
    and my family
to find out what others think of my ideas.
I can join in a class brainstorm or a group topic.

Research

I have written down what I know about my topic. Here are the questions I want answers for.

I can write about news at school, in my community, in New Zealand, and in the world.

I can interview people, and write about people who interest me.

mum went shopping and got some pizza. A long came Greedy Robbie. Munch Munch Munch and that was the End of that.

Adaptation

I can use known structures and innovate.

I can take oral language and turn it into writing.

I can rework previously written drafts.

Other people's suggestions

I can get ideas from the teacher and explore new kinds of writing.

I can write something a friend or my family has asked me to write.

Finding ways to continue

When I'm not writing, I don't have to wait for the teacher—I can search myself for things to write about.

I can write a review of last night's TV programme, a film I've seen, or a book I've read.

I can write the instructions for a new game I've just learned.

I liked the book about volcanoes the teacher shared with us. I want to find out more.

I can write a newspaper advertisement to find Jimmy's lost cat.

I can fill in my diary.

I must make Mum a list of things to take on the school camp.

Daydreams

I can talk, scribble, or let my mind wander to generate new ideas.

The teacher's role

Knowing their children

The teacher's role in choosing topics is to know and value their children's interests, experiences, uniqueness, territories, feelings, and what is significant in their lives. Topic choice should, as far as possible, be left to the writer although in some situations, such as reporting on a science experiment, the choice of topic is restricted. However, the range of subjects in the curriculum offers plenty of freedom for learners to generate their own topics.

When learners choose their topics for themselves, they retain ownership of their writing, and have a purpose for writing. Most children at the early levels are full of ideas which they can write about. But teachers should show that sharing the task of choosing a topic is helpful and important, especially for anyone suffering from "writers' block".

Patricia Grace says:

> *Your world is where you are and what you listen to, and your experiences are things of value to you as a writer. Sometimes young people don't always realise that. I hear them saying, "Oh, I couldn't be a writer because I'm boring." But nobody lives in a vacuum—there's something going on about us all the time; there's something going on inside us all the time.* [22]

Stimulation

"Writing floats on a sea of talk."[23] Teachers should encourage learners to talk to them and to each other about their choice of topic. There will also be many opportunities during study in different curriculum areas for teachers to suggest writing topics. At times, the whole class will be involved in their own writing about one topic. But teachers should always be prepared to accept that a learner's topic choice may be a better idea than the one they themselves had suggested.

Modelling

Teachers themselves need to be active writers, with all the genuine challenges that this entails. They need to model choosing topics and, giving reasons for their choices, to write on a variety of topics.

It is helpful if teachers keep their own topic list as well as encouraging the students to keep one.

Focusing on and interpreting the topic

Teachers need to show that some topics just don't work out. Sometimes the topic choice is too wide for the writer to handle successfully. Teachers should encourage writers to frame a "working title", which may be changed at any time. For example, a focus may emerge as the scope of the ideas becomes clear, or a more appropriate title may be chosen after the writing is finished.

When topics are set for writers, it is important to clarify what exactly is to be discussed. Writers should attempt to clarify, or at least state their interpretation of the topic or question, before beginning to write.

By respecting their students, teachers will encourage them to make their own decisions on what to write about, and how to set their own research questions, thus enabling them to be independent writers.

Conferences

When learners seem stumped for something to write about, teachers might help them to extend a recent topic by asking questions that:

- reorient the topic in time and space;
- place it in a hypothetical situation;
- personalise it;
- give it a more specialised purpose.

Reorienting in time or space:
Did you find out how it worked? Have you thought of explaining that?
What happened to the others before that/after that/while that was going on?
Was it the same last year? How was it different?
Where did that circus/person/animal come from? What was it like there?

Placing in a hypothetical situation:
Do you think your friend/mother/sister/neighbour might have a different idea about that?
Would that be the same if you were grown-up/from another country/in another country/a boy/a girl?

In your story, you talked about taniwha from the deep sea. If human beings lived at very low depths, how would they have adapted to survive? Have you ever thought what a deep ocean person would look like?

Personalising a topic:
Has anything like that (having a plant wither/experiencing gas escape under pressure as in a tyre blow-out/being in an earthquake/floating on water/being bullied) ever happened to you/ someone you know?
Could you write that as a story now, or as an article? How will you start a story/an article?

Giving a topic a more specialised purpose:
You wrote about the new bike/camera/skateboard you got for your birthday.
Do you know how to fix it if something goes wrong with it? What *can* go wrong with a bike?
You wrote about the new kite/chocolate cake you got for Christmas. Could you write the instructions for another person to make one like it?
You told me about your trip to the beach.
What might a scientist/doctor/nurse/diver/businessperson want to know about that?

we did mesring at mafs
w mesred our wasts
with wol. mrs DiKSeinS
waSt waS the BgeSt
and GonnaS was the
smll St

Learning through choosing different topics for writing

It is important that timetable constraints and professional divisions do not isolate genuine writing experiences in one area of the curriculum, or at any one time of the day. As every subject area makes use of language, especially written language, in learning about new topics, an exchange of teaching strategies and objectives between different curriculum areas is not only desirable but essential.

Determining the Audience

Writers should speak first from their own experience and knowledge, in their own voice, maintaining their integrity. However, writers need readers, so they must consider their audience unless they are to end up writing only for themselves.

In discussing their purpose for writing, they will consider *how* they are to communicate successfully with their chosen audience. Students in class will usually be affected by an immediate response from their peers, but they should also consider the possible responses of an unseen audience.

> *The only important thing in a book is the meaning it has for you.*
> Somerset Maugham, *The Summing Up*

Key learning outcomes

In determining audience successfully, learners will:

- have clear goals, and know how these will affect their writing;
- feel that what they will write is valuable and interesting to others;
- expect to respond to, and profit from, others' responses and writings;
- distinguish between public and private writing, and the effects of audience on content, clarity, and expression;
- expect to receive help from the teacher, from others, and from examples of writing for different audiences.

The learner's role

Learners ask, "Who is my audience? What do I want them to know?"

Defining goals

I can state who I'm writing for and what I want them to know.

I know why I am writing.

I know my purpose will affect the way I write.

I can say why others would want to read my writing.

Feeling valued

I think my topic is interesting.

I know I can say something useful and interesting about it.

Valuing others

I like to hear my readers' responses.

I like to respond to other people's writing.

Public and private writing

I know others will read my writing.

I can read my writing to others.

I can read other people's writing.

I know that writing is private sometimes and won't get to an audience.

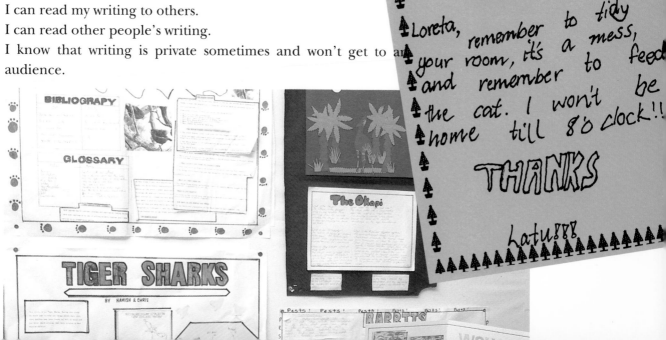

I know that writing for others is a way of recording and clarifying my ideas.

Getting and giving help

The teacher will read many examples of writing for others.
I will discuss my audience with others.

The teacher's role

Modelling

It is up to the teacher to demonstrate the need to write for a purpose. When the audience is clearly defined, it determines the way the writing is crafted. Sometimes the writer has no special audience in mind—when writing a poem, for example. Here audience plays a lesser role in shaping language.

Conferences

The teachers should expect the children to be able to describe their purposes for writing, and should provide them with opportunities to reach their intended audiences.

Writers need time to talk to the teacher, their friends, their group, and their class about who they are writing for, and whether they are getting their message across in an interesting way. Only by discussion, gathering information and ideas, and planning how to order and present them, can they consider their audience fully.

Teachers should ask learners to think through who their audience is by asking quite specific questions such as, "Who are you writing this for?" "Who is going to want to read this?" "What age are they?" "How well do they know you?" "What do they do for a living?" "What do they do in their leisure time?" "How much do they know about it?" "What do you think they want to know/need to know about this?" "What sort of things do you think they will be used to reading/reading about?"

Teachers will not ask all these questions of all learners. They will not need to. Crucial questions will depend on what the teacher is aiming to help the learner achieve concerning facts, forms, or presentation.

Learning through writing for different audiences

Writing for an audience, especially one which knows less about the topic than the writer, or presenting information in another more suitable form, makes use of study skills, deepens understanding, hones ideas, and makes the communication more precise. All this is especially useful in clarifying concepts and extending study skills in curriculum areas.

Finding Out, Selecting, and Ordering Information

The issues here are to help students realise three things:

* what they already know about a chosen topic;
* how they can go about finding out more;
* and how they can organise their information into a coherent plan for writing.

> *The writer cannot build a good, strong, sturdy piece of writing unless he has gathered an abundance of fine raw material.*
>
> Donald Murray, *A Writer Teaches Writing*

Although research material can be arranged to make drafting and composing easier, the main shaping force should be the purpose for writing, and the need to communicate to the intended reader what is useful to them in the clearest and most interesting way. However, not all writing is done from a collection of notes and references.

Key learning outcomes

In finding out, selecting, and ordering information successfully, learners will:

- recognise what they know and what they need to know;
- feel ready to seek and find further information;
- feel satisfaction in discovery;
- make use of both spoken and written language in extending and evaluating information;
- order and focus information for a selected audience;
- make use of appropriate study skills, techniques, and tools.

The learner's role

Learners ask, "What do I know about the topic? How do I order my information?"

Self-confidence

I know something about this topic.

I know I can find out more.

Seeking help

I can seek help and comment from:

the teacher;

my friends;

my family;

the community;

other sources of information, for example, the Town Hall, the public library, or the visitor centre.

I can talk to myself.

Pleasure in discovery

I like asking questions about something I don't know. I can ask, Who? When? Which? Where? How? Why?

I like finding out the answers. I can ask, "What was the cause? What was the result?"

Reflective talk, writing, and drawing

I can verbalise as I draw pictures or diagrams, or jot down ideas.

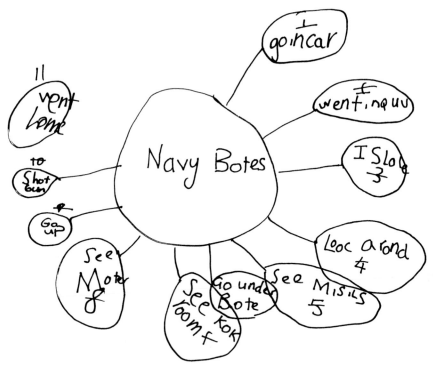

I share ideas and discuss them to make my meaning clearer.

I can explore my topic systematically.

I can write an outline of what I am planning to say.

I evaluate information by testing and checking what I have found out.

Replanning organisation and focus

I know if the ideas in my notes are relevant.
When I am faced with new, or too much information, I can refocus my topic. I can put new information in the best place.

Keeping audience in mind

I ask myself if I have ordered my ideas in the best way for my readers.

Study skills

I can gather and search for information, and have skills such as:

    reading for detail;
    skim reading;
    finding things in the library;
    recording sources of information;
    cross-referencing;
    interviewing;

Passovers / resource number

Question		Resource	Page	Graphic
How it's celebrated	1	Passover Lynne Scholefield	7-12	
	2	Sari's Passover	20-20^{24}	Picture
What preparation is required	1		7-8	
	2		20-22	
Why it's celebrated	1		8-9	
What traditions are followed	1		7-12	
	2		12-19	
What's a seder meal	1		18-26	Picture, diagram x 2.

experimenting;
observing;
questioning;
problem-solving;
making notes by:
    paraphrasing;
    summarising.

Tools and techniques
I can use pen and paper/chalk and blackboard/tape cassette/word processor.

The teacher's role

Finding out about prior knowledge
The teacher's main task is to help children discover what they already know about the topic and clarify their understanding of it. Teachers need to talk to the children and to encourage them to share their knowledge and their writing with each other. They should help learners to pose questions for themselves and others to answer.

Time to think and plan
Learners need the chance to improve what Tizard and Hughes call their "intellectual scaffolding"[24]—the structures through which they organise their ideas of the world. Teachers need to encourage them to question, select, and order information from a variety of sources.

In a skilled writer, the process of gathering information often overlaps with planning its use in subsequent writing. Learner writers usually need to repeat this kind of organisation at successive stages.

> *. . . while teachers at this level [form 2] encouraged students to prepare a topic and to generate or gather ideas, instruction on how to organise the ideas was often lacking . . .* [25]

Modelling
Teachers need to demonstrate the skills of gathering and organising information.

For example, in gathering information, teachers need to show how useful it is to draw pictures or diagrams, make jottings, and take notes to clarify meaning and record knowledge. Other techniques for gathering information can be taught as they are needed. They include, for example, the use of topic sentences, common abbreviations, quotes, numbering and heading devices, noting down references clearly for future use.

Finding out more often involves going to people and talking to them. Learners need to practise polite but searching interview techniques. The ways in which young learners may approach and question their elders, and record their responses, will vary from culture to culture. It is often best for teachers to seek advice from their community if they are unsure about ways of guiding the learner.

Students also need to be shown how to summarise textual material. They may have tagged a passage in the research stage, but now they should realise the importance of passing the information through their own minds by paraphrasing it in words that make sense to them, rather than copying it out verbatim.

Whatever techniques are taught, the ever-present questions in the student's mind should be, "What does this mean? Is it relevant here?" Being able to discard unnecessary information is a skill that needs practice. Stressing the need for well-focused writing is of great importance.

Organising information

Teachers can model how to organise information by demonstrating simple techniques such as using upper or lower case letters for headings of different importance, using colour, circling, numbering with Roman, Arabic, and lower case letters to show sub-divisions or subcategories. These techniques are not always obvious to students. Grouping techniques, such as noting items on small cards or slips of paper which can be easily re-arranged may also need to be taught. Teachers can help students find out about how language is used to arrange catalogues, indexes, and data banks. Many students will be using a computer to access and order information. They will be learning about the technology of information handling.

Making logical connections

As Linda Flower says, "One of the most common yet most demanding kinds of real-world writing people do is expository writing, or writing that analyzes or explains." This skill develops when emergent writers draw a picture and make a logical connection between that and what they have written.

As writers develop, the free association of ideas may be noted down in a "brainstorm", but these ideas need to be mapped or structured in some way to give them shape. Making connections between ideas, analysing and classifying them, and putting them into some sort of order can often be done through a "semantic web". This may be a first step towards sequencing ideas logically. In dealing with complex material, putting ideas into some sort of hierarchy and showing logical connections can create a well-organised plan for future writing. Both these systems for ordering ideas are illustrated below.

The ideas in the semantic web are connected but not organised into a hierarchy. One well-tried way of structuring ideas is by means of a tree diagram. Teachers might take a semantic web and show learners how to work with their ideas so that minor ones are gradually classed under major ones, finally creating a satisfactory plan for writing. Often this will lead to a more manageable focus for the writer, or belated inspiration may change their direction entirely.

First ideas are jotted down in a brainstorm.

The ideas are grouped into categories in a semantic web.

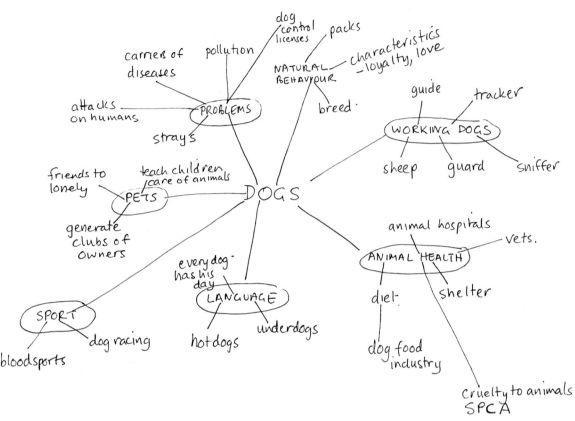

The writer's questions and discussion act as a focus from which notes are made. These show that there is too much material.

Questions

1. What is my focus? Have I a title?

2. what do I know about this topic?

3. What must I find out?

   (who, when, which, why, where, how often, what if ......? — questions)

4 Can I make a tree diagram?
   Shall I alter my focus?

Answers.

1. Our friend the dog
   Man's best friend.

2. Care   expense (food, shelter, vet.)
   exercise   - ask Mum & Dad
   characteristics   - our dog
   breeds?   - our dog
                     - get a book on other kinds
   benefits to me - what about old people?
                              lonely people?
   Working dogs - lots of things they do.

3. Check breeds
   Find out what sniffer dogs sniff
              which dogs find people in avalanches
              what training is done for sheep dogs
                    "   "   "   "   "   guide dogs

4 TOO MUCH !!!
   Cut this down to dog control.
   New title   Man's Best Friend ???
   Make a tree.

The writer selects and focuses the topic more clearly in a tree diagram.

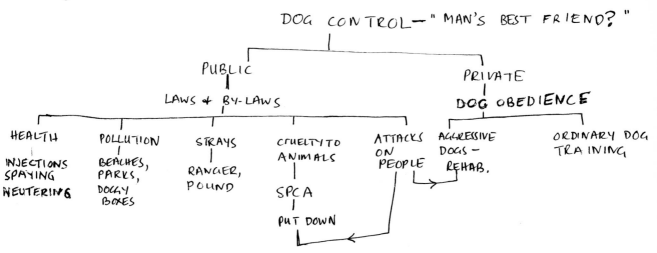

Conferences

Teachers should not underestimate what a learner knows about a topic. Sometimes learners are unable or reluctant to define experience. They need help to recognise what they already know as something worth writing about. Specific questions (who, what, when, where, which, how often, why) may help to place, supplement, and extend experience. Teachers should not be too quick to assume that silence means that the learner has no answer to such questions. Wait time is often proportionate to reflection or shyness.

Talking ideas over with others often helps enormously to clarify sequence, logical development, exciting twists of plot, and so on. Although discussion is not only about the order of the information, recognising a logical development of ideas is especially important for a learner-writer. Often the writers have not expressed all that is necessary to communicate what they wish to say about a topic. It is important for them to realise that the reader has only the words on the page to work with. Encouraging learners to talk with each other often makes the gaps or confusions clear.

Ideas which do not easily fit a selected category of fact or information may need to be placed through the teacher's guiding questions so that thoughts begin to show some kind of pattern , for example, "Had that happened before?" "Who/what else has done that?" "Where else has that been seen?" "What was the result of that?" "What caused that?" "Is that the same as the other, or different?" Learners can be helped to define, compare, contrast,

45

contextualise, and seek causes and effects, using their supporting evidence. The teacher in this way may help to control the learner's focus of attention.

Learning through ordering information for writing

Helping writers become conscious of form is the major task in this stage of the writing process. This applies not just to the understanding of the characteristics of different genres (see pages 49-53) but also to what makes an example of structure within a genre good or bad. Sequencing, relevance, and logic are important aspects to develop, as are the use of contrast, comparison, example, and recapitulation to make meaning or emphasis clear. When learners organise their information for a purpose, they often create their first real understanding of their topic.

This aspect of the writing process offers most opportunities for the development of appropriate study skills. Information one cannot access or make use of is merely "noise".

Any piece of knowledge I acquire today has a value this moment exactly proportioned to my skill to deal with it.[26]

Learners will need to be critical about the "facts" they discover from texts, interviews, or other sources. These will all need to be correct when the writing is published.

Appropriate Forms

Experience in different genres, structures, and styles, and their emotional effect on the reader is gained over many years. Giving learners many examples, and allowing them to determine a form appropriate to the chosen audience and purpose, prevents overly directive teaching from stifling the writer's voice.

We can think of a genre as a social process, i.e., as a particular set of activities or a way of doing something. . . . these activities are carried out for some purpose. This is true of any genre; it is a social process which has a purpose—some goal that people are working towards. It also has a recognisable structure or pattern. Finally, a genre is something that arises within a particular culture: it is a product of the culture.

John Collerson, *Writing for Life*

Key learning outcomes

In handling appropriate forms successfully, learners will:

• know about the characteristics of different genres;
• structure their own writing, within a genre, soundly and effectively;
• recognise differences in voice, register, and style;
• write in a variety of genres, forms, styles, and register.

The learner's role

Learners ask, "How can I put my information into an appropriate form?"

Forms

I know my teacher will show me many different forms.
I can discuss my choice of form with my friends.
I have increasing control of different forms such as:

  poem,
  letter,
  diary,
  play,
  dialogue,
  caption,
  story,
  cartoon strip,
  article,
  notice,
  summary,
  paraphrase,
  notes,
  instruction,
  hypothesis,
  explanation.

I can select a form to suit my audience.

Structure

I know that my writing shouldn't ramble on.
I want to move my ideas and information around to shape my writing.

I have techniques for grouping jottings and ideas.
I have techniques for sequencing ideas.

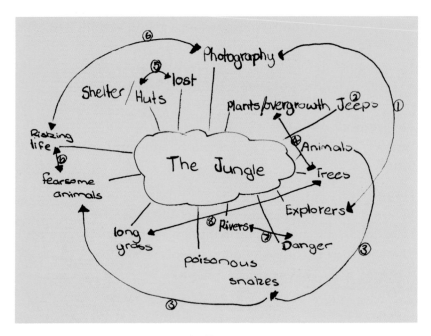

I like working out causes and effects.
I am getting better at structuring my writing.
I can see when writing is badly structured.
I can analyse the structure in others' writing.
I can analyse different forms of prose.
I understand that fact and fiction are structured in different ways.

Style
I will experience many different authors' voices in my reading.

I am beginning to experiment with appropriate styles.

Register

I know I will vary how I write according to:

who I am writing to;

what I am writing about;

the occasion on which I'm writing.

The teacher's role

A definition of terms

See the Glossary, page 128, for a discussion of the terms "genre", "register", "form/structure", "style", and "voice".

A general category of writing may include different forms. For example, the text in an "article" may be a piece of continuous prose, but in a photo article, text may be short captions. A piece may also be well and clearly developed (have good **structure**), or poorly arranged (bad structure).

All writing, too, bears the stamp of its author. The author's **voice** or **style**, or the structure in which they write, may be affected by the chosen form—for example, by the form of a letter—or the current fashion. And the **register** of the author's voice will also be affected by the character of the interaction between them and the person they are writing to—the tone of a letter of congratulation to an old friend will differ from one of formal complaint to an official.

Modelling

The children need a wide experience of the many different forms which writing can take. It is often not sufficient to expect children to generate forms intuitively. They must be consciously taught. This can be done by reading to the children a variety of genres and styles of writing, and discussing them to discover their characteristics.

Hilary Lamb's research into writing performance in New Zealand schools[27] showed that narrative was the foremost kind of writing students practised. There was little emphasis on the kind of writing that argues a case or presents a viewpoint ("expository or transactional writing"). So sometimes teachers will need to direct the kind of writing to be attempted to enable their students to gain a particular experience, or practise a particular genre[28] (for example, report rather than narrative).

Today we have a frog in our class room. We saw the frog. It was on top of the lid. They are tappoles first. Then they turn into frogs. They are little frogs. They have no rocks in the aquarium. They will soon
by Sariah?

Relation Ship between Lester and
Relationship Clyde.

After Lester thought about the way
he was treating Clyde. (but he hid)
He started feeling sorry for him self but he
had rights too. He kept looking for a pond
he said, "It is too hot!". frogs don't like pond
heat!" He found a pond and he jumped in
Splat! He cried out for help but nobody

Frogs <u>Article</u>

By Takeng

Frogs (Are) have stickey dicks
under there fingers & toes.
The most poisnes Toads of
all,
is the Cain Toad.
Frogs wsely hide inn bushes
and Trees.
Frogs eyes and nostrils.
are on top of there heads,
So they can breath and swim
in the water.
Some like to Leap (on a)
for like the R.P.

INTEVIEW / The eating stages of a Frog.

Reporter: "Mr frog, I'm from the Hutt valley reporters college, my first assignment is to interview a frog about it's eating stages, I was wondering if you could help me?"

Mr frog: "sure, I'll be glad to."

Reporter: "Mr frog, when you were still inside your egg, what did you eat?"

Mr frog: "Well, that was a long time ago, it's amazing I still remember, I simply ate the yolk of my egg, it's quite delicious for your first taste."

A Life Cycle of A Frog

The Female Frog lays some eggs.

The Tadpoles turn into a frog.

The eggs hadch.

Then they grow front Arms.

The Tadpole eats its Shall.

The Tadpoles grow feet.

The Tadpoles look for food.

Giving learners a framework should not be done so rigidly that it hampers them from developing their own voice and meaning. In clarifying their own material for an audience, learner-writers will move naturally towards appropriate forms. In the best writing, there is unity between content and form. For example, assist learners to write *as scientists* from their own experience, rather than *about science* by copying others' explanations. (Students often believe that the act of copying makes the material their own.) By trying to communicate understood ideas clearly and logically, learners approach the best kind of scientific writing. George Goldby says this of transactional and expressive (personal, attitudinal, or affective) writing:

> *[If] science is primarily a process of personal observation and investigation. . . . then observing, thinking and investigating in science should be articulated not through transactional but through expressive writing which—like the work—is both personal and exploratory.*[29]

If learners, therefore, have been exploring science as a process of investigation and discovery, rather than a passive acquisition of others' knowledge, their way of working will be reflected in their use of language. From their first largely expressive writings, once their knowledge is secure, learners can begin to communicate it in an appropriate expository form.

Note that scientific, expository writing is a genre in which the writer's voice is still heard in what is described. Even though words expressing feelings are often avoided, to describe an event as a *plague* of locusts indicates the writer's attitude or personal experience.

Can I turn a crayon into a candle?

What happend

I put a crayon in some boling water to make it soft I left the room for a minute I came back in to took at my expererment and the crayon had nearly melted this ment that the crayon I was going to use would not work for my experiment So a new experament

Teachers need to be familiar with many different forms that writing can take. Narrative has its own special forms, and these vary between cultures. Teachers should be aware that, while all stories illustrate alterations in events or characters, or both, not all offer resolutions to a problem, or follow the same pattern of climax and anti-climax. The beginnings, middles, and endings of fiction and expository prose also differ.

Texts often have multiple meanings. Readers may perceive a text as different genres—some may read a story as a straight yarn, while others may see deeper or hidden meanings in it. Readers construct their own psychological reality of the text according to their experience in language, and their important concerns.

Writing on several levels is something that writers mature into, but at early stages learners can be shown different perceptions of the genre of a text—*Gulliver's Travels* is a classic example of a text that functions as a political text or moral tract as well as a narrative. Aesop's fable of the Hare and the Tortoise, Biblical parables, or Hilaire Belloc's *Cautionary Tales* illustrate the same concept.

Conferences

Writers need to talk to themselves and to each other about the best genre for their writing. The teacher needs to encourage the children to talk with each other and share their work.

Teachers could say, "Now that you know what you want to write about, what is the best way to do that/most persuasive way of getting that across? Why?" A clear picture of audience should guide the writer here.

Writing in another cultural pattern also presents a significant challenge. Writers who are using a second language may break taboos in English inadvertently. Writing in the patterns of their own language, they will use traditions, forms, and registers which are appropriate for them. As styles and structures of writing vary between cultures, teachers will need to be sensitive about how they approach apparent infelicities. Guidance could be gained from local community members.

A teacher says of her Pacific Islands students:

They write differently; they've got a slightly more circular style. . . . I do think that there's a difference in the way it goes on paper and the way it's thought through, and I've got to be sensitive to that, to get the best out of them. I find that aspect of writing and language very interesting. [30]

Learners in group conferences may comment on the use of vocabulary and style. They should be shown that their comments need to be qualified. It is not enough to say, "I like the way you ended your description . . . "—there must be a reason—". . . because you gave us a little summary of all you had said." Teachers will have modelled this type of response in discussion with children during shared or guided reading, and during their own writing done in front of the class or group.

An example of a group conference:

David   (reading to the group) If there was ever a cunning animal, it is the fox. Down through the ages man has marvelled at his cunning. The fox is a cousin of the dog. It has dark red fur and lives in a home called an "earth". Although members of the same family, dogs and foxes are mortal enemies, and dogs have been used for hundreds of years to hunt them down.

Marie   Am I right in saying that man has marvelled at how cunning foxes are?

David   Yes.

Marie   Why is that?

David   I think it's because they have so many ways of being able to escape from dogs and other enemies. Hunters used to say, "As cunning as a fox".

Wendy   I see. I think you could have that bit in your article.

Tina   I liked the way you wrote about being cunning. What made you use those words?

David   I don't know. I think I must have heard it in a book somewhere.

Learning through writing in appropriate forms

Taking a story or play or article and re-presenting it in another form is a useful way of enabling writers to see how form and meaning affect each other. The same content may succeed in two different forms but whatever form is chosen, it will, by its very nature, affect the *content* which is expressed. A poem on hunger could properly contain material which would be excluded from a science description, and vice versa.

Composing and Drafting

Getting it down on paper—revising it as you go

The composing and drafting stage of the writing process covers two apparently conflicting aims.

The first is the need to write fluently, speedily, crashing through technical barriers such as handwriting, spelling, and punctuation, and getting things down as best one can from one's plan.

Second, is the over-riding need to convey ideas successfully, involving playing with words, testing them to their utmost for clarity and inventiveness, wrestling with them and their meanings to enrich expression and make communication work.

Composing and drafting are the constant flux of creation which closes in on the author's meaning, and through which the author's voice emerges.

> *Words should be an intense pleasure just as leather to a shoemaker.*
>
> Evelyn Waugh, *The New York Times*, 19 November, 1950

> *The intolerable wrestle*
> *With words and meanings.*
>
> T.S. Eliot, *East Coker*

> *Revision is the process of seeing what you've said to discover what you have to say.*
>
> Donald Murray, *Learning by Teaching*

In the world of publishing outside school, this process of shaping to make meaning clear, which can involve major restructuring of the text, is done either by the author on the publisher's advice, or by an editor. For the learner writer at this stage, the focus is on *revision to make meaning clear*. It is in this capacity that learners are attempting to create "the shadow of a reader". In this context, "editing" is synonymous with "revision" or "drafting".

Key learning outcomes

In composing and drafting successfully, learners will:

- internalise the information gathered and present it in their own words;
- use revision strategies effectively to improve communication;
- develop their ideas and feelings in a well-formed structure;
- make effective use of technical aids, for example, dictionaries and word processors;

- evaluate the accuracy and effectiveness of what they have written;
- seek and profit from the on-going responses of others;
- recognise and negotiate the time necessary for a particular task.

The learner's role

Learners ask, " How can I make my writing clear and effective?"

Creativity and clarity

I am ready and willing to get on with my writing.

I understand that quality of expression is more important than length.

I search for the word or phrase to best express meaning.

I arrange words and sentences to create effect.

I consider the logic of ideas and their development.

I make use of technical aids such as a thesaurus or dictionary.

Ownership

I can understand what I have found out, and have put it into my own words.

Revision and expansion

I search for more information, and revise my writing to cover gaps in detail.

I add, delete, reorder, and remould my writing.

I use revision strategies (see page 60).

My new Cat

I'm geting a new Cat today I want a female I want a fortise with lots of wight shell and I'll call her emma. I got a new cat today but... it wasen't a tortise shell, it didn't have lots of wight and I can't call her emma but but I love him anyway

Word processors

I can use a word processor instead of a pen to:

write the first draft of my story;

shift, cut, or add to text;

retain copies of previous drafts for possible use;

revise and remould within the sentence;

compose tentative versions;

try out possible layouts and consider their implications for text.

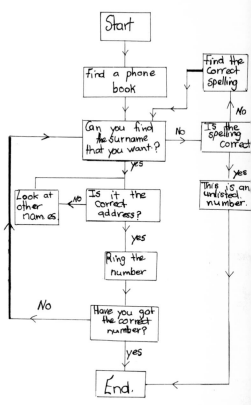

How To Use A Phone Book.

Graphics

I can select ideas which are best presented visually, and present them, for example, as:

illustrations,

flow diagrams,

tables,

graphs.

I relate text to diagrams through captions and headings.

I consider the best placement for graphics.

Self-evaluation

I have learnt to stand outside my writing and ask, "What have I said? Does it make sense? Will the reader understand? Have I shown bias? Have I said what I think? Are my facts correct?"

Seeking response and responding to others

I read to the class or group, and expect questions about and responses to my writing.

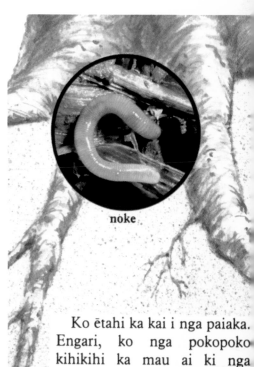

noke

Ko ētahi ka kai i nga paiaka. Engari, ko nga pokopoko kihikihi ka mau ai ki nga paiaka kia ngote ai te kauri.

57

I continually share drafts during writing to clarify my meaning.
I seek, accept, reject, defend against, and take notice of the responses of others.
I expect the teacher to ask questions.

Pacing oneself

I take time to review and reconsider.
I negotiate time for composing and drafting with the teacher.

The teacher's role

Modelling

The teachers should write in front of children and demonstrate the need to clarify meaning. They should model the types of questions that help writers to revise, and expect children to ask these questions of each other and of themselves.

They need to demonstrate ways in which information can be reordered, reoriented, changed, deleted. They should show honestly that, although writing is fun, it involves hard work—writing a quality piece takes time!

> *It's miles better if teachers of writing do write themselves. At one stroke, you remove barriers if you do. It puts you both in the same world.[31]*

Writers who are new learners of English may need special help in getting their ideas on paper or on the screen, but like beginning writers, they should be "writing" their own text from the start if possible. The practice of circling or marking any words these learners are not sure of can become established once they have understood that written words have spaces between them. Beginning writers should have the opportunity to "read" their text to the teacher, who will provide a correct written model where necessary.

I've got a (spo s l) (bagl.
my nano (gva) it to me.
It's a (slva) (bagl.
I like it   I wer it to
School.

Approximations in spelling

Donald Graves stresses that children need to be able to write freely without interruption to their thoughts. Allowing children to attempt spelling enables them to use vocabulary from their oral language which then flows on into their writing. Spelling is functional—it enables the writer to express meaning. It is, therefore, a tool for writing, not a barrier to the writing process.

Focus on meaning

The teacher should convey that clarification of meaning is the pivot of revision in writing.

On the completion of a draft, the writer has revised by:

• adding and clarifying information;

• reordering;

• deleting or replacing words or phrases.

The writer:

• is satisfied with the way the writing is structured;

• sees that those responding to the writing are understanding the intended message;

• knows that drafting and revision of writing are concerned with meaning;

• as far as possible, has checked that the facts presented are correct;

• knows that writing will not be perfect—up to this time, concern has not been primarily with surface features and spelling.

Throughout all this, writers should be satisfied that their own voice is clearly present.

Conferences

Many opportunities should be provided for writers to talk in groups, in pairs, and with the teacher (see page 104 for a description of different kinds of conferences). The sharing of ideas with sympathetic listeners is most helpful in clarifying one's own thoughts.

The teacher needs to train the children to reflect on what they have read or heard and then ask questions about text which are focused on making meaning clear, for example, "You said it was missing—where did it really go?" "You said it was sort of green—what *exactly* does that mean?" " You said you might have liked it—how did you really feel?" "You said that Brian didn't smile—what did he think about it?" "You said it made them fall over—was that the real reason that happened?"

Strategies for revision

Students who drafted their work on a word processor will find one especially useful at this stage of the writing process. But learners can be shown many techniques with pen, pencil, and paper to make composing and drafting easier. For example:

* writing revisions in the margin space;
* writing on every second line;
* dividing the page (two thirds for writing, one third for revising);
* revising by reordering paragraphs (cut and paste);
* lead-writing (experimenting with opening paragraphs);
* experimenting with concluding paragraphs (often the hardest part of writing);
* hunting for the right word (replacing one word with a better or more appropriate one).

Learning through writing and revising drafts

Putting things down in writing is the ultimate challenge in conveying meaning without ambiguity. Learners will find that things which are familiar to them—for example, how a bumble-bee flies—and which they believed had been communicated successfully to others, are unclear to the reader. The discipline which writing imposes is an illumination. It is up to teachers to pace this discovery so that it does not become a disenchantment.

> *Writing is, par excellence, the activity in which we consciously wrestle with words in order to discover what we mean. The process itself unfolds the truths which the mind then learns. Writing informs the mind, it is not the other way around.*[32]

Correcting and Publishing

Correcting and Proof-reading

Respect for the audience now guides the writer's effort. In composing and drafting, the writer's attention was focused on making the meaning as clear and forcible as possible. Now words, spelling and conventions of punctuation, facts, quotations, references, diagrams must all be checked, and corrected if necessary. Any text which is to be read by others should be correct.

This final correction of learner writers' texts by the teacher is called "editing" by many but does not, at this stage, involve re-structuring of the writing. That should have been done during the revision stage. In the context of correcting, "editing" is synonymous with "proof-reading".

Reading maketh a full man; conference a ready man; and writing an exact man.

Francis Bacon, *Of Studies*

Poor spelling in the midst of a good piece of writing is like attending a lovely banquet but with the leavings of grime and grease from the previous meal still left on the table.

Donald Graves, *Writing: teachers and children at work*

Key learning outcomes
In correcting and proof-reading successfully, learners will:
* show respect for the reader by applying what they know in correcting text;
* show independence in doing their own proof-reading;
* develop competence in spelling and using surface features.

The learner's role
Learners ask, "How can I make my writing ready for a reader?**"**

Respect for audience
I know that readers expect everything to be perfect and factually correct.

I am willing to proof-read my work to show respect for the audience.

Independence
I know that the teacher expects me to proof-read as much as I can by myself.

As I develop some skills, I use a red pen to show the proof-reading I have done for myself.

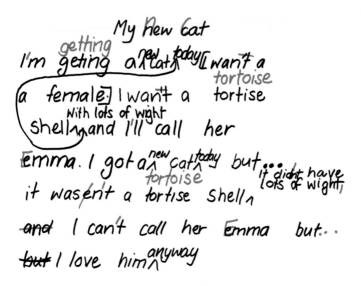

I expect the teacher to praise me for doing my own proof-reading. I like to hear what the teacher has to say.

Making use of modelling

I expect the teacher to correct everything I don't yet know about. I know the teacher will provide a correct model.

Skills

I feel good about my growing list of skills—"I am learning to . . . /

I can . . ." I expect to develop effective proof-reading skills.
I am willing to take risks and make approximations. I am able to self-correct some of my spelling approximations—I am developing a "spelling conscience".

Seeking guidance

I know the teacher will help me determine what to learn next.

I know the teacher will not overload me with new learning.

I will proof-read as much as I can, but I am willing to let the teacher finally check and correct any work to be published.

The teacher's role

Respect for the reader

The teacher needs to demonstrate respect for readers, and to instil that respect in writers.

Modelling

Teachers should encourage writers to correct as much as they can for themselves. They can do this by modelling proof-reading, and talking out loud, especially about surface features in their own writing, or by drawing attention to the correct use of surface features in published material.

The teacher should finally see that everything in children's writing is correct for publishing, but the writer, after discussion, should have the last say so that the piece is in their voice and not the teacher's.

Conferences

Children need feedback on what they are able to do so that their next learning step makes sense to them. This next step should come directly from the child's current piece of writing.

Donald Graves comments:

> *Make it a discipline to choose one thing to teach, realizing that retention from conferences is high. The tendency when first working with conferences is to overteach, since the teacher feels it may be a week before she meets with the child again. Overteaching means the child leaves the conference more confused than when he entered.*
>
> *After several months, conferences can be shorter because both teacher and child know how to function together. Remember to expect children to speak first about three things: "What is the piece about, where are you in the writing, and what help might you need?" When children speak first, much time is saved.* [33]

Individual conferences, therefore, now concentrate on providing writers with feedback on what they have corrected for themselves. Teachers should then identify and teach an appropriate skill. This may be correcting an aspect of punctuation, recognising a spelling pattern, identifying an appropriate relationship between visuals and text, or establishing methods of checking facts.

Any necessary resources for correcting, such as a dictionary, thesaurus, a source for facts, examples of conventions of surface features, and so on, should be to hand.

Spelling

The following section is based with permission on Richard Gentry's paper, "An analysis of developmental spelling in *GNYS AT WRK*".[34] (See also Bissex, Select Bibliography, page 142.)

Teachers need to develop their own understandings about spelling and learning to spell so that they have intervention strategies which meet the needs of individual children, leading them towards correct spelling. Richard Gentry states (page 199) that "...learning to spell must be treated as a complex developmental process. . . . As teachers observe spelling skills unfold, they must engage pupils in the kinds of cognitive activity that lead to spelling competency."

Gentry has identified five stages of spelling development:

1   precommunicative—in which the child uses symbols from the alphabet to represent words;

2   semiphonetic—the child's first approximations in represent-

ing letter-sound correspondence;

3   phonetic—the child represents the entire sound structure of
the word being spelled;

4   transitional—the child moves from relying on sound to represent words to relying more on visual representations;

5   correct—the basis of knowledge is firmly established, and further experience results in finer discriminations.

Precommunicative

At this stage, the child:

- shows some knowledge of the alphabet through the production
of letter forms to represent the message;

- shows no knowledge of letter-sound relationship, with letters
strung together in a random way;

- may have an understanding of the left to right principle of
directionality;

- possibly includes some number symbols;

- may repeat a few, or make use of a substantial number of,
alphabet symbols;

- frequently mixes upper and lower case letters;

- generally prefers upper case letters in early samples of writing.

Richard, aged five, " I am going in the train to Masterton with Mum and Dad."

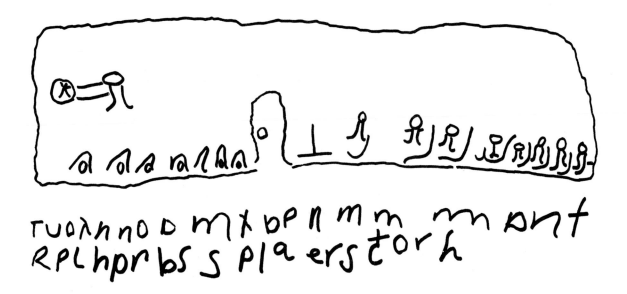

Semiphonetic

At this stage, the child:

- begins to grasp the idea that letters have sounds which represent the sounds in words;
- provides a partial phonetic representation of the word being spelled, with only one, two, or three letters being used, for example, "w" (went), "wk" (walk), "BZR" (buzzer);
- makes use of letter names to represent sounds or syllables, for example, U (you), R (are);
- begins to grasp the left to right principle of directionality;
- gains greater control over alphabet knowledge and letter forms;
- may make use of spaces between words.

David, aged five years four months, "I went for a walk."

Phonetic

At this stage, the child:

- provides a total mapping of the letter-sound relationships in the word being spelled;
- develops particular ways of spelling certain details of phonetic forms, for example, nasals before consonants, — "bangk" (bank), "stingks" (stinks);
- assigns letters strictly on the basis of sound, without regard for the conventions of English spelling, for example, "sed" for "said";
- generally makes use of word spacing and the left to right principle of directionality;
- shows a mixture of stages, with some words spelled phonetically, some semiphonetically, and some correctly.

Roshan, aged five years ten months, "When school finished, I went to the library. My Mum said to me hurry up and I found some books."

wed sk/ was finsd I wnt to
the Libee my mm sed to me haRee up
and I fwnd Sum bKs.

An example of an individual conference on spelling at the phonetic stage:

Teacher	What are you writing today, Jade?
Jade	Tommy and I broke the kitchen window.
Teacher	Oh no! How did you do that?
Jade	Tommy kicked the rugby ball and I missed it.
Teacher	What did Mum say?
Jade	She took my football away from me and said I've got to wash the dishes for a month.
Teacher	Unlucky you! So what have you got so far?
Jade	Tommy and I . . . (Jade pauses.)
Teacher	How will you spell broke?
Jade	I don't know.
Teacher	Say it slowly and listen to what you can hear.
Jade	br-o-k
Teacher	What can you hear?
Jade	k?
Teacher	Great! Where does that come in the word? You listen: br-o-k.
Jade	At the end ?
Teacher	Great! Put it down. Now let's listen again and see if we can get the start.

Jade picked out the "k" because it was the last sound he heard. This is quite common. If Jade cannot get the "br", the teacher will try to associate these sounds to a known word.

Teacher	It's like "breakfast".
Jade	"br"?
Teacher	That's right. What two letters say "br" in "breakfast"?

If Jade cannot get any more letters correct, the teacher may write in the rest of the word.

Teacher	What comes next? Read it again.
Jade	Tommy and I broke . . . the . . .
Teacher	You can write "the" and have a go at "kitchen" for yourself. I'll be back soon.

Transitional

At this stage, the child:

- undergoes a transition from a great reliance on sound to represent words to a much greater reliance on visual representations;
- uses vowels in every syllable, and makes use of vowel combinations such as "ai", "ea", "ay", "ee", "ow";
- uses both vowels and consonants instead of letter names, for example, "el" rather than "l" for the first syllable in "elefant" (elephant);
- represents nasals before consonants, for example, "end" rather than "ed";
- uses the silent "e", as in "tipe" (type) in contrast to "tip" (tip);
- makes liberal use of learned words and common inflectional endings such as "-est", "-ing", "-ed", "-s", "-ies";
- shows the movement from phonetic to visual spelling strategies, for example, "eightee" instead of "ate" (eighty);
- includes appropriate letters but reverses the order of some of them, for example, "huose" (house);
- uses alternative spellings for the same sound, for example in, "eightee" (eighty), "lasee" (lazy), "rane" (rain), "sail" (sale).

Joshua, aged six years four months, " Stanley is going to the vet today to have a needle, and he is going to stay the night there, and Stanley climbs trees and bites toes."

Sanly is going to the
vet today to Hav
a neeble and He
is going to sta
the niet thre

and sanly Climbs tee
and Bits toes.

Correct

At this stage, the child:

- accumulates a large body of known words, including the correct spelling of prefixes, suffixes, contractions, compound words, and forms derived from the Classical/Romance languages, for example, "addition", "precious", "poetic";
- shows growing accuracy in the use of silent consonants, for example, "climb", and doubled consonants, for example, "hopping";
- understands that some words which sound the same (homophones) have different spellings according to their meaning, for example, "eye" and "I";
- is able to suggest alternative spellings when words "don't look right";
- gains growing control over irregular spellings;
- has effective control of spelling resources such as a dictionary and a thesaurus.

Traditionally, spelling instruction has been a formal lesson and the memorising of lists of words often unrelated to the child's own writing. There is sound evidence to suggest that many children do not automatically transfer learning from a formal spelling lesson into their writing. There are, however, indications[35] to suggest that spelling generalisations are enhanced when spelling is regarded as a skill of writing, and individual, group, and class programmes are structured accordingly.

While the importance of the message contained in the writing is paramount, the work of emergent writers is slow and halting, as they cope with developing handwriting skills and concentrate on the conventions of spelling. With appropriate intervention by their teacher, children will develop sound-letter associations and increase their confidence in their ability as writers.

At later stages, approximations in spelling continue to be made by writers as they express more complex ideas. Teachers need to identify those approximations which are close to the correct pattern and build on this knowledge, leading the child to competency.

Being able to identify when a child is ready for new learning and what should be modelled is the mark of the experienced teacher. For some children a particular point may need to be modelled over and over again. For others, once shown never forgotten. Identifying the teachable moment is something of a lottery, but by using a knowledge of what children are able to do, and what is developmentally appropriate, a teacher's intervention should be considered and planned in more than just a casual manner.

It is not, however, only through the teacher's intervention that the child learns about letters, sounds, and correct spellings. There will be many other opportunities, including reading books, observing other writers, interacting with the language around them in all its forms, and listening and talking with others, where this knowledge will also develop.

Some word processor programs provide valuable help in learning to spell unknown words as well as checking spelling. Students should also be well supplied with dictionaries and be encouraged to use both these tools.

Learning through making writing correct
Making a text completely correct is often an arduous job. Time needs to be allowed for learners to achieve objectives. These will vary according to the writer's stage of development, but at any stage the learner should be encouraged to attain accuracy in some respect.

Publishing

New Zealand educators have noted that where publication has not been part of the writing programme, or has been treated in a casual manner, there has been a general lack of interest in writing. The programmes lacked impact because no purpose and audience had been determined for the writing. As a result, children tended to see writing as a neat copy produced to order. Classrooms that allowed children to negotiate time to reach a published form of work seemed to achieve higher overall standards of writing.

> *There is no reward so delightful, no pleasure so exquisite, as having one's work known and acclaimed by those whose applause confers honour.*
> Jean Baptiste Molière, *The Would-be Gentleman*

Key learning outcomes

In publishing successfully, learners will:

- be keen to select and publish their work;
- make use of design in the effective presentation of text;
- take the audience into account;
- seek and give responses on their own and others' text layout;
- use a variety of publishing media, forms, and styles;
- make good use of available resources in materials and time.

The learner's role

Learners ask, "How can I publish my writing?"

Sharing with others

I am keen for people to read my published text, and am eager for the response of a variety of readers.

My New Cat

I'm getting a new cat today.
I want a tortoise-shell with lots of white.
I want a female
and I'll call her Emma.

I got a new cat today...
It wasn't a tortoise-shell,
It didn't have lots of white,
I can't call her Emma but...

I love him anyway.

Design

I am keen to shape my writing into an appropriate and attractive form.

I am able to plan the layout of text, using what is known about how text is set out.

I take my audience into account in my design. I can set out my text so that it is easy to read.

Getting and giving help

I can collaborate with others.

I know that the teacher or others, if necessary, will provide a correct text.

I seek feedback from others about my plans.

Different media

I use a variety of illustrative styles to enhance and clarify meaning.

I know there are many ways to publish, and am keen and able to use a variety of publishing forms, such as:

   cassette tape,

   chart,

   book,

   poster,

   article,

   display.

Resources

I know that the classroom has all the materials for publishing.

EMERGENCY PREPAREDNESS QUESTIONNAIRE

Q. Where is our meeting place in a disaster?

Q. Do we have a survival kit? Why / Why not? If we do where is it?

Q. What is in the survival kit?

Q. How long will it last?

Q. What does our family do when a disaster strikes?

Q. Do you bother to grab anything during a disaster?

Q. Do we have a plan for what I / the children do when a disaster strikes? What is the plan?

Q. What happens when nobody is at home during a disaster?

SURVIVAL KIT

Water — Games — map — Torch — Can food — Pass Port — books — Fire Works — good shoes — Blankets — $10 $10 $10 money — Warm clothes — Batteries — Toilet Bag — strong gloves — Rubbish bag — matches — candles — Bags

... to have a survival kit in your home ... an emergency strikes. your survival ... Save your life. It may take several ... the Civil Defence is able to help you.

MY BODY

My body is brown
My tongue is pink
My pants are blue
My feet stink
My heart is red
My bones are white
My muscles are as strong as dynamite
Some peoples feet are the same as mine
But my shoes are size nine.

Robbie Vale

Favourite Toys

AWAKERI SCHOOL
New Zealand 1990
MAGAZINE 1990
By Daniel Butler

Techniques

I can write or type my own material.

I can use a word processor and printer.

I can make use of art techniques in shaping my work.

Time

I am selective about the degree to which I shape material which is going to be published.

I negotiate appropriate time with the teacher for the shaping mode (publishing).

The teacher's role

Negotiating time

Publishing is an important part of the writing process. Learners should be allowed time to publish their work in a form appropriate to the purpose. For instance, a note to a friend may be read in its initial form but a published booklet on "Jungle Animals" will be much more elaborate.

Good and successful published writing is not done in a minute. Learners need to know that they have time to produce a piece of work they can be proud of—time to research, think, question, take notes, draft, revise and edit, proof-read, and publish. Time is important to all writers at every stage of development, and too much can be as bad as too little. Learners should negotiate publishing deadlines, otherwise preparing a work for publication might run on for too long at the expense of composing and drafting new text.

Handwriting and word processors

Publishing involves skill in handwriting. But handwriting, like spelling and punctuation, is a tool of writing. It enables the learner to put ideas down on paper in a way that others can read. Children's ability to write legibly should not be confused with their control over the writing process. Handwriting should not be seen as something to be developed before written language, but rather as something that develops alongside it.

The development of handwriting skills is explained fully in the appendices of the Department of Education supplement to the primary English syllabus, *Teaching Handwriting*.[36] Difficulty with the mechanical skills of handwriting should not be allowed to hinder children's development as writers, where technology provides a means by which these children can become independent.

The development of handwriting skills from new entrants to Standard Four.

Today is Monday.
It is a cloudy day
12 E4 567890

Mrs MUIS NaVl

Iq.mgoina toq zzies+t
silverstreem

Iamgoinhgtotheshop.

The light-house stood or
cliffs. There were rocks
foot of the cliffs. The
boats could see the lig
from a long way out

The sun was shining brightly on
the morning of the big day, but
the ground was still white with
snow and the air was very...
Outside the ...
enormo...
hered t...
ket hold...
ment wa...
before ten... the crowds were
pushing and shouting, and police.

They are now found all over New Zeala
along the coasts, on the islands, in tuss
country, on farms and in city garden

75

Many children have access to word processors. Their use is not only in publishing but also in drafting and revising text (see pages 55-56).

Modelling

Teachers need to ensure that children are immersed in a wide variety of published models. They should also demonstrate a wide variety of published forms in their own writing. The importance of the quality of the words should not be lost in the business of presentation. Although good visuals can lift a mediocre text, students should not spend so long on presentation that they neglect to think about the text itself.

Style and register affect both words and visuals. Text for a poster will differ from the same content presented in a brochure. For some forms of text, space or absence of visuals is the best option.

The message is put in the short, rhetorical form of a slogan.

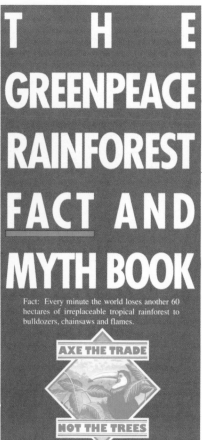

The message is summarised in punchy, short statements.

```
Dear Supporter,

In the minute it takes you to read this page, another 60
hectares of tropical rainforest will have been destroyed.

Does that sound impossible?  Believe me, it's not a typing
error.  Over 85,000 hectares of tropical rainforest around
the world are destroyed every day.  (That's an area
half the size of Stewart Island).

If this orgy of destruction continues, the world's tropical
rainforests will virtually disappear by the year 2000.

                    The ques
                    stop des

It's devouring 100 mil
of species, 1000s of h
into the atmosphere 30
global warming, and ch
patterns we all depend on

Driven by money, corruption and
developers, and the land-grabbe
tree in the last forest is fel

That's why, at Greenpeace, we
international tropical rainf
reforming the trade in trop

And that's why I'm writing
urgent support.
```

The message is sent in a friendly, relaxed style.

The message is as brief as possible.

76

Teachers can draw learners' attention to the range of texts publishing involves—acknowledgments, blurbs, copyright permissions, indexes, contents pages, and so on.

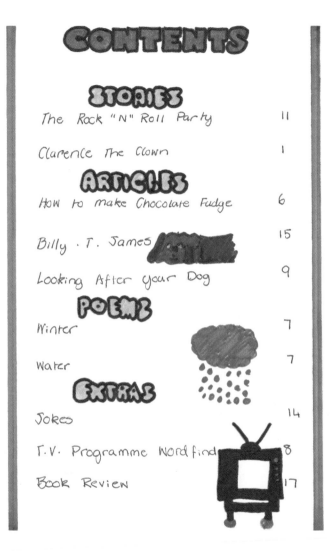

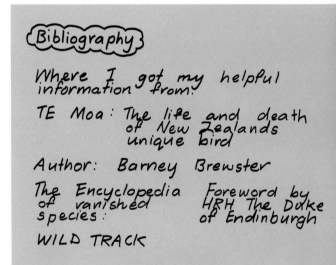

Quality and independence

An understanding of the writing process will help children produce a quality product, and will support them in trying out their own ideas and publishing methods.

Resources

Children should be provided with all the necessities to produce a quality product. These are both human and material—for example, parents, typists, the teacher, other children, paper, art materials, typewriter, word processor, and printer.

Conferences

In many cases the medium for the writing will have already been decided on at the stage of forming intentions. But now discussion relates to the layout of text. Questions now centre on:

- how response to meaning is affected by presentation;
- the sizes and type of fonts to be used;
- how illustrations and diagrams relate to text and captions;
- the effects of highlighting by the use of boxes, space, or bold text;
- what sort of breaks or divisions are in the best interests of the reader;
- what headings are to be included, and where.

Concerning this last point, the shape, content, and meaning of headings and sub-headings, their relation to the text, and their effect on the reader will be a point of importance and interest to the writer.

Finally, the actual materials, sizes, or colours for the publication will need to be discussed, and use and ease of access considered.

Preparation of final text can and should be done by all possible and appropriate means—handwritten, typed, done on the word processor, written out for the learner by an adult. The learners do as much as possible themselves, and adults step in where needed.

Learning through publishing writing

A look at modern publishing shows how much the presentation of material affects the reader's response. Publishing means that learners will be combining the arts of graphic design with their language abilities—their visual literacy will be important. This is an opportunity for language teachers to work across the curriculum, joining forces with, for example, the art or science teacher, or exploring the many different media in which we present information in the modern world.

Note that the visual meaning attached to graphic symbols in one area of the curriculum may not be the same as their meaning in other areas. An arrow can stand for movement through space or time, but can also indicate change from one form to another. Teachers should be sure that such symbols really describe what the writer wants to say.

Outcomes

Audience Response

Once a work is in a published form, opportunities must be made for the writing to reach its intended audience.

As the writer seeks the response of readers, much learning takes place. The writer learns to accept justifiable criticism with equanimity, and profit from it; the reader learns to present points without offence, backing them up with evidence. Readers will gain different perceptions of the text according to their backgrounds, opinions, and state of knowledge. This should be taken into consideration when the teacher is guiding discussion.

But most important of all—both readers and writers need to learn how to give and receive praise for the quality of message, as well as for effort and presentation.

Teachers need to recognise the importance of developing language and social skills.

They have the right to censure that have the heart to help.

William Penn, *Some Fruits of Solitude*

Key learning outcomes

In responding to others' writing, and profiting from others' responses, learners will:

- readily share their published work with many others both in and outside the classroom;
- be eager to read the published work of others;
- expect a response to their published writing;
- see the purpose and value of publication and response;
- react positively to others' responses, making appropriate adjustments to their own writing;
- offer constructive criticism with courtesy and understanding.

The learner's role

Learners ask, "How will my audiences respond to my writing?"

Opportunities for sharing

I know the teacher will :

make time for me to share published work;

(with my permission) read my writing to the class.

I know my writing:
   will be displayed;
   may be collected into a class anthology;
   may be catalogued and put in the school library.
I know my family, and others in the school, will read my writing.
I look for opportunities to share my published work with a wide audience at other times.
I want to read others' published work.

Expecting responses

I know that readers will respond to my writing.
I see publication and response as one of the purposes for writing.

Making responses

I listen and read attentively.
I convey comment positively by explaining clearly why the comment is made, and suggesting alternatives.
I know the value to others of genuine praise.
I am aware of, and respect, points of view and approaches different from my own.

Reacting to responses

I know that there will be time to reflect on my writing experience.
I feel good, and want to continue to develop as a writer.
I am confident in processing responses and regard this as a means of learning.
I have discovered, from people's responses, what makes communication work.
When my target audience does not respond, I search for reasons.
I gather new ideas for writing.
I show an increasing desire to revise my work, and feel responsible for proof-reading it.
I respect other points of view.

The teacher's role

A supportive environment

The teacher should provide an environment where responding to writing is a natural part of the development of text. Some students may prefer to say nothing rather than appear critical. But, by demonstrating appropriate responses to writing, the teacher will show the same respect for learners' writing as for already established writers. Teachers should be ready to accept constructive criticism from their students, demonstrating that a quality response can improve and motivate further writing.

Reaching the audience

Teachers need to provide opportunities for learners to reach their intended audiences. Responding to each others' writing is a great spur to language development. Learner-writers' favourite reading is often the work that they and their classmates have produced.

Cultural considerations

Teachers need to be sensitive to cultural ways of expressing criticism. It may be best for students to present their material to a small group, to have a friend to support them in their presentation, or even to present the material on their behalf. Some students may be particularly shy about standing up in front of others. Teachers need to lay down clear guidelines for peer comment (see the advice on group conferences on page 106).

Conferences

Presenting one's work so that it may receive a fair response, and coping with a group's reaction to it, is a fairly daunting experience even for an accomplished writer. A set of routines will help students respond constructively to another's writing.

Writers should not apologise, praise, or excuse writing before readers have had a chance to read it; readers should share the response time, respond to the main issues in the text before the details, and keep on-track during discussion. Everyone should make a verbal comment, which should be balanced, including both praise for good, and advice about weak, passages.

Comments on texts need not be restricted to group conferences. Published writing may be taken home, and people may write a note about what they have enjoyed in their own and other children's writing.

The most successful comment that can be made on a writer's work is for others to read it by choice, and with enjoyment and profit.

Learning through responding to writing

Facing up to what others think of you is one of the great challenges in life. A writer bares his or her soul when sharing writing. Learning to respond without offence, and yet with guidance, is a skill of inestimable value. It can only be done if the audiences make an attempt to inform themselves about both the writer and the subject. Through acute questioning and discussion, readers and writers learn more about the subject involved as well as the qualities of good writing.

Conclusion

The main purpose of education is to offer not just more of the same but more at a higher level, as learners themselves improve their own performance and enhance their own knowledge—good teaching is forever being "on the growing edge of the child's competence".[37]

> *Human learning presupposes a specific social nature and a process by which children grow into the intellectual life of those around them. . . . the only "good learning" is that which is in advance of development.*
>
> Lev Vygotsky, *Mind in Society*

To enable learners to "grow into the intellectual life" around them, teachers need to focus attention on what the learner is trying to do. Teachers and learners need clear goals. But teachers should pace the steps learners need to take to reach these goals so that they are attainable within a stable social and emotional environment.

Teachers also need to set things up so that learners can *recognise* ways to solve their problems, with help where they need help, but freedom when they can manage on their own.

Jerome Bruner calls this "upping the ante"—raising the level of what has already been achieved by stretching it towards what is to be achieved.

Creating good writers means creating good thinkers—language and intellectual growth go hand in hand. Appendix 1, pages 121-4, details the criteria by which one can judge the development of learners' thinking and writing at three broad, overlapping stages. However, the basic question for teachers to ask of students' writing at any stage is:

"Can these learners communicate their understanding of their world?"

4

Young People's Writing

What do young people write about? What is good writing? How can teachers help learners dance with a pen?

The Ministry of Education has published three journals of young people's writing by inviting students to submit scripts. Among the large and enthusiastic response were examples of every type of primary school writing from junior classes to Form 2. Here, John Bonallack, the editor of the Parts 3 and 4 School Journal and the Journal of Young People's Writing, himself a primary teacher, talks about what he found in his mailbag.

If you go mushrooming, you walk through many barren fields, but when you find one mushroom there will usually be others around. So it was when reading through the thousands of contributions submitted for the *Journal of Young People's Writing*. Where there was one outstanding item, there were often other examples of fine writing in the batch from that class or school.

This confirms what is well known: that certain teachers, practices, or situations stimulate and foster good writing; that writers are made, as well as born. This chapter looks at examples taken from work by children, and at factors in the writing that make it more, or less, effective. (Pages 118–20 gives some guidelines for value judgments on the quality of learners' writing.)

Writing from experience

Children almost always write best from their own experience. The closer children are to a real experience (and that closeness may be a matter of intense feeling rather than time), the more sharply and specifically they will write, and the more lively the story is likely to be.

Hey, guess what! Today one of our teachers was almost killed. Well, she could have been killed if she'd been standing a bit further back. We were all in the hall for. . . [38]

That account is alive, even if the teacher almost wasn't.

Accurately observed and remembered detail brings to life this description of a sea crossing:

> *When we got out on to Cook Strait, the ferry was rocking like mad and people were being sick all over the floor and into their Cheeseball packets.*[39]

I have shown the story this comes from to several groups of children and said, "What do you remember best?" Each time they've chorused: "They were being sick in their Cheeseball packets!" A line like that is not something a writer could have dreamed up. Children's accurately observed detail is almost always more effective than their invented images.

Further on in the story, the writer shows that same talent for observation and description when he describes finding a sea slug.

> *It swam like a snake moves, and its skin started pulsing up and down like a balloon being blown up. As soon as I picked it up, it squirted a powerful jet of water at me. It had tentacles on its underside, and big warts all over it. It felt like a balloon filled with water.*

This is expository scientific writing of the best kind—a simple, clear observation of phenomena, but including what adult science writing often omits: the feel and the excitement of the thing.

Listening and remembering

In retelling experience as narrative, it is not only visual detail that makes the text come alive— it's also the words that people say. (These can be remembered or, better still, noted down at the time.) Dialogue is an excellent short cut to character, as in this excerpt:

> *When we got home, Mum said, "How was it at the races?"*
> *Dad just grunted.*
> *"What did he say?" Mum asked me.*
> *"Oh, he's mad because he lost $20 on Bonecrusher."*
> *"He what?" said Mum.*
> *"Lost $20," I said.*
> *"That silly oaf," said Mum. "Oh well, it's his own fault."[40]*

That's real people speaking! It is good writing because, by recording natural speech and preserving the voice of the character, the writer has evoked them far more effectively than a description of similar length could have done.

Creating shared experiences

All children have experiences that can be tapped, but it is often worth creating a shared experience that a class can discuss, write and read about together. Role play can serve as an "experience". Children are naturals at entering roles—it is one of the ways they learn to find their places in society. It shows in their play, from the five-year-old's "Let's say . . ." to the thirteen-year-old's "dungeons and dragons" simulation games.

In the gathering momentum of an extended role play, the shyer children are often freed to express themselves in honest and vivid ways. One class spent two days in costume and role as English immigrants coming to New Zealand in the 1860s. They were

promised housing by the Company agent, but after spending the night in the school hall (done up as an immigrant ship), were given instead a pile of manuka, twine, and canvas, and expected to make their own accommodation in the drizzle. There were arguments over who would get the best piece of land; alliances were formed— and betrayed. Later, the children were able to write with feeling about the experiences of "colonial settlers".[41]

It's an ear for dialogue and the experience of role play that prepare children for writing drama—a form that they often have little experience of at school. In fact, very few plays were submitted for the *Journal of Young People's Writing* by young writers. Some—and it was often those with a Maori or Pacific Islands heritage—showed a talent for writing in dialogue, and it can be a simple matter to translate this sort of writing to play form.[42]

Elaborate role plays like the immigration episode aren't always necessary. Any class trip will provide experiences. After a visit to a park with a water slide, one child wrote:

> *. . . on my fifth go, I thought it was fantastic. My thought was, "I never*

The language of fantasy

Writing from personal experience produces excellent work, but so can imaginative writing. Original fantasy is a rare treasure in children's writing, especially in older children's work. It should be nurtured. These pieces by young writers show the freedom of thought the young are blessed with.

> *There is something under my bed. I looked under my bed last night and I saw its eyes. When I go home tonight, I know there will still be something under my bed.* (a 7-year-old)[53]

or

> *Once I saw a dragon dancing down the street, dribbling jellybeans out of his nose. He said, "Want to dance?" "Yeah! I would!" But as we danced, he dribbled jellybeans all over me. I laughed.* (a 6-year-old)[54]

As children, particularly boys, get older, such fresh images from the mind become rarer. Instead, their taste in fantasy often turns to haunted houses, graveyards, space battles, Egyptian tombs, war, retellings of violent videos, and "dungeons and dragons" style stories. The unsophisticated ones usually start along the lines of:

> *It all started when I was walking to my friend's house. On the way I saw a haunted house . . .*[55]

or

> *One day while I was riding in my space ship , aliens attacked me. I fired my laser guns . . .*[56]

The language and structure can be more sophisticated, and at times sickeningly violent.

> *"Take cover!" yelled the sergeant as he dived into the shrubbery. Sylvia caught her foot against a tree root and was pounced upon by a barrage of gunfire. She was hit in the thigh, the stomach, and one bullet shattered her left elbow. Sylvia screamed in pain and felt the comfortable wave of unconsciousness drift over her.*
>
> *Sergeant Thompson pulled his Browning automatic out of its shoulder holster and fired twice. The first shot plummeted into Mark's kneecap, the second hit a tree. The machine gun was out of his grasp, so Mark's hand went straight to his Luger, and he fired in the direction of Sergeant Thompson. This caught the sergeant off guard, and he was hit in the lower*

> *hip. Alistair grabbed the sergeant's partner's .45 Colt out of its holster and pumped a full chamber of lead into . . .* [57]

and so on, a total of seven close-typed pages.

This is formula writing, macho style. From the girls there were far fewer stereotypes, but formula romance weddings did feature in several stories:

> *The veil was of delicate chiffon. The dress had puffed sleeves; the bodice was very tight and fitting, and showed off the girl's slim figure excellently.* [58]

And from a girl who was obviously a keen follower of royal marriages:

> *Carefully and daintily, they walked up the aisle to where Prince Edward and Simon were waiting patiently, stunned by the beauty of the dresses. "Kneel and take your vows," said the Archbishop.* [59]

Such writing may serve a purpose in the development of a child's self-image but, as fiction, it only rises above the stereotype when the author is exceptionally gifted. Children need to be told that while their stories of this kind may be fun to write, they are often not fun to read. Their writing of this sort is measured against professional commercial writing—and it usually contains the same overused content without the technical skill. It is also virtually impossible to write a satisfying adventure or romance on the grand scale—something that more properly belongs in a novel—in a few pages.

There is also the "slick" writing particularly prevalent among forms one and two boys. Again it is influenced by the language of comics and popular cartoons and is designed, not to communicate, but to hide the writer's feelings. This is "safe" writing, that draws on a casual style and a quick laugh. It is likely to be endorsed by the writer's peers, and once established in a classroom, it spreads like a weed.

> *Quackula, after escaping from jail, walked down the cobbled street wondering what to do next. He soon arrived at an old castle. On the drawbridge there was a sign saying: KEEP OUT. THIS PROPERTY BELONGS TO MACHO DUCK, YA DIG??** Quackula was furious (and thirsty too) so with his magic finger he lowered the drawbridge and stormed in. When he got inside, he hung up his coat on a coathanger, and Boob! Boop! an alarm went off! Macho Duck came scrambling down the stairs with an orange sub-machine gun . . .* [60]

There was a predominance of this sort of writing in the over three thousand submissions for the first *Journal of Young People's Writing, Some Place Wonderful.* Presumably it reflected a trend in classroom writing which teachers had either encouraged or been unable to avert. Of the stories, over half were adventures of the war or haunted graveyard type. None made it to the final selection. Not so much from prejudice; they simply didn't stand alongside the excellence of the personal experience writing, the poetry, and the small amount of original fantasy. For subsequent issues of the Journal, very few war-type adventures were submitted. The selection in *Some Place Wonderful* had determined to some extent what young people wrote (or, at least, what they sent in). In the classroom, also, the kind of writing children produce will largely be determined by what the teacher chooses to endorse.

To the children who send their adventure stories, hoping to have them published in the Journal, I usually reply, "Your best chance of being published is to write **simply and honestly about something that has mattered a lot to you**. Writing in that way, you can have an edge on professional authors, because only you know exactly how you feel, and you are also closer in age and experience to young people who will be reading your work."

Expository writing

Children can and do tackle expository writing—writing that gives a reasoned argument, or sets out to instruct or inform. It is often a part of writing from personal experience—the description of the sea slug on page 86 is an example—or this child's comments, following his zoo-school work with endangered animals:

> *One of the hard things about doing this job is that we know what actually happens to some of these animals—how they die. We've seen videos of it, and it's horrible. It's awful that humans can just walk into animals' homes with a gun, and the animals have got to try and escape—till one day, they don't.[61]*

It can also be generalised from specific personal experiences, as in Joseph Harris's treatise on tangi:

> *When a Maori dies, the body is put in a coffin and taken to a marae or kept at their house. It usually stays there for three days. If it is in their home, the family clears the room of all furniture, knick-knacks, and beds. They*

put mattresses around the walls of the room, and put the coffin in the middle. The main family sits around the body and stays there most of the time, even to sleep.[62]

Poems

Poetry is an attractive form for young writers. Their poems are usually short, and get straight to the point. Children enjoy experimenting with rhyme, but unfortunately, the need for a rhyme often determines the direction of a line, even the whole poem, and can reduce the result to doggerel.

Race day is drawing near,
Exciting moments might appear.
Oh, look, there's one ahead.
One is orange, one is red.
They call it Swordfish I think.
One of them is going to sink.[63]

Sometimes a promising beginning can be spoilt for the same reason, as in:

Water is a funny thing,
It has no shape, but it can sing.
It sings as it rushes down the river . . .

Great, so far, but then:

. . . And if you like, you can make it quiver.[64]

Students can be shown that poetry in English depends on form, metaphor, and rhythm more than on rhyme. Note that the poem, "Not Me" (quoted on page 92) has no rhyme in it. In the following poem, there are suggestions of rhyme, but the writer has not been constrained by it:

Some Place Wonderful
Perhaps there is a line
Somewhere in time,
Between falsehood and make believe;
Maybe there's a time
In this world of mine,
Where everything's as you please.
Perhaps for a moment
The grass turns purple,

For a moment so short that no one notices,
And when you see a boat
Floating in the stream,
Maybe that boat is us.
Maybe there is a moment
When you're half asleep,
That it is drawn closer,
And perhaps if at that instant
You reached out a hand
You would touch an angel,
And you would be carried far away
To some place wonderful,
Somewhere lovely and beautiful.[65]

If too great a reliance on rhyme can produce poor writing, so sometimes can copying form. Forms such as those based on the initial letters of a theme word can be a useful way of getting reluctant or unconfident writers started, but they rarely produce memorable results. If an idea works as haiku, that is probably because it is a succinct and self-contained idea, not because the author found the shape useful to fit a big idea into. Better that students say what they want to say, and if they are accomplished enough to do it in poetic form or rhyme, that is a bonus.

Writing it out of yourself

Occasionally, writing is cathartic: a piece that is written primarily to get something out of one's system, or to face up to, or take control of a feeling. It is unlikely that this work will be intended for reading out in class; it may not even be meant to be read by the teacher. It is understood that some work is not for publication; just through the act of writing, the piece may have served its purpose. Although submitted for a *Journal of Young People's Writing*, the following was probably not originally written for publication:

> *He had no right to rape that woman. That's how I feel about my uncle.*
> *I hated him for what he did to that woman, and to our name . . .*[66]

However, there is always the possibility that a piece of cathartic writing is trying to communicate something sincere, or even desperate, to you as a responsible adult. The response here will be to the child's cry for help, not to the literary content of the writing.

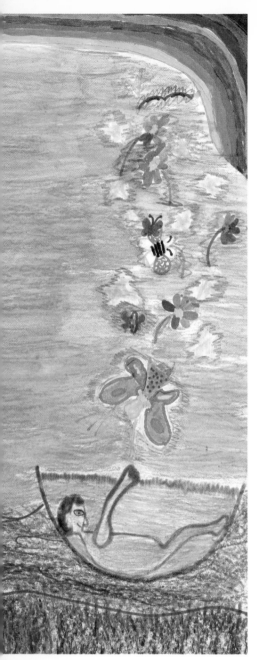

Writing for a purpose

Finally, children need to know that writing is for a purpose, and that it is a criminal waste of time to write rubbish.

Hello, I'm a little lunchbox named Jerry.[67]

began one submission for the *Journal of Young People's Writing*.

As an editor who has read thousands of submissions for the *Journal of Young People's Writing*, I would ask teachers not to put children in a position where they are writing simply to please, or to produce "at least two pages". Rather, give them experiences to write about. Give them a purpose for writing. Give them the skills to produce literate work. And give them publication opportunities inside and outside the classroom, and a readership to appreciate their work.

The same young person who wrote "Some Place Wonderful" (see page 96), while attending an extension class, wrote:

The tunnel of writing stories was boring to me till that day when I was introduced to the class, when I came to a fork in the tunnel—as soon as I turned right I took a step up. When he opened the door a crack, I rushed and took a peep in, and I longed to go in and I did. It was an escalator. An escalator of skill and of joy.[68]

Never underestimate the ability of children to write, nor the power of a teacher to put them on that escalator of skill and joy.

Note: All the examples except one are by students of primary school age—from junior classes to Form 2. Because they have been gathered over a number of years, and the young writers and their teachers have in many cases moved on, it has not been possible to get permission to use most of these excerpts. All published quotations have been credited to writer and source; the unpublished ones are left uncredited. We trust that the authors will accept their use in this way in the interests of fostering writing in schools.

5

Organising for Writing

Classroom organisation

Writers are as diverse as writing. The way, therefore, in which they are managed needs to be flexible. Teachers will need to create the groupings, spaces, and times which enable children's writing and reading development.

There will be many occasions when the teacher demonstrates or models a particular strategy, convention, or form to the whole class. This may arise from an identified need for some members of the class. In modelling good writing techniques for *all*, however, those who are already confident will have their knowledge confirmed, and those in need of direction will have the opportunity to learn. For example, this whole-class activity could range from modelling speech marks to learning about the most effective ways of reviewing a film. As learners attempt these techniques for themselves, there will be a need for small group or individual teaching.

As well as teaching for the very young learner-writer, and overseeing the development of writing in all areas of the curriculum, teachers will need to consider the needs of learners whose language competence, cultural background, and previous educational experiences may not match what they are asked to do. They may need special help in acquiring the language of the curriculum. Their ways of working and understanding will be different. This book has not tried to address such issues in detail, but reminds teachers that care may be needed.

> *[Teachers'] approach to children as learners can be gained from observing how they organise the pupils in their classroom.* [69]

A Stimulating
Writing
Environment

A typical organisation

Writing occurs daily in most New Zealand classrooms. A typical organisation tends to be a workshop model, with teachers setting aside half an hour or so per day for writing, during which time they model writing, conduct individual or group conferences, and make time for sharing and responding to published writing.

The writing workshop is a good starting point for teachers who are learning about the teaching of writing, or for beginning teachers trying to establish themselves by using a structured lesson format. In many cases, however, there has been a move towards integrating writing with a wide range of learning experiences. This shift in direction has not come about because of dissatisfaction with the workshop style of organisation but through growth in teachers' understanding of the links between reading and writing, and listening and speaking. As a result, children are using their writing skills consciously in learning how to learn in many areas of the curriculum.

It should be stressed that there is no one way to organise for writing. While a range of teaching strategies is suggested in this book, there is no thought to promote one organisation as superior to another. The form of organisation used should contribute most to the learners' development.

Routines and timing

In any approach, there are many different forms of writing activity going on at the same time. Not all children will be writing, or publishing for that matter, simultaneously. Learners will be spread through the process. Some will be engaged in forming intentions, others will be drafting, using pencil and paper or a word processor. Some may be thinking about or discussing their writing, while other children may be proof-reading their work. A few will be working with the teacher, or engaged in publishing. Those with finished text may be sharing their work with an audience. In this situation, the demands made on the teacher's time are spread. Teachers will be able to work with individuals, and monitor them as they write. Organisational difficulties occur only when all the children require assistance at the same time. This also applies to the use of shared resources such as the listening post or word processors, which will be needed for different purposes at different times. Good routines in which the learners feel secure, flexible use of time, and a predictable management structure are important in developing good writing programmes at all levels.

Time is important for the learners, too. They should know that they will have time to write without pressure, and that they can work this out with the teacher. They should expect to write regularly, on their own , with a friend, or in a group, and take it as a matter of course that they will write in all subject areas. When learners are put into groups, the type and size of group should suit their present needs. If they do not see the reason for this grouping, it should be explained to them.

The social environment of the classroom

Learners in a relaxed atmosphere, who know the routines, will write better.

The atmosphere of the classroom will have a powerful effect on whether they are willing to share their writing with confidence. They should know that the teacher will always be ready to listen to them, and that they and their friends like to read and discuss what they write. They should know that the teacher expects them to behave with consideration for others, especially younger or more timid ones, or those from another cultural background. This may involve making routines for sharing clear to them, and demonstrating and practising the language of polite argument and discussion. Teachers who are not certain of differing cultural patterns of interaction should ask community members or the advisory services for help. It may be quite inappropriate, for example, to pair a boy and a girl in a buddy system, even though they have the same language background, or to split up children apparently too dependent on each other without finding out how their families or community members have required them to behave.

Classroom resources

There should be much writing and reading material all around— many different kinds of paper to write on, many books to look at and consult, always paint, glue, brushes, paper, scissors, and anything else needed by learners to give their writing an interesting look. There should be easy access to a word processor, a listening post, records, and tapes—in languages other than English for some of the learners.

Places

Writing is not something done at only one time and in one place. Learners should realise that they can work in many places—the reading and writing areas, the science and maths areas, the science and maths rooms, and in other rooms, too. They should be allowed to sit wherever they prefer **as long as they behave co-operatively**. Those who want to concentrate on their own may wish to work in a carrel, others may wish to move their desk to work where it suits them best. All learners should know where to go to talk over their writing when they need help.

Conferences

Conferences, above all, should aim to increase the writers' confidence in their own voice. Learners should expect to talk things over with the teacher (or others) before, during, and after writing. The successful teacher of writing uses the writing conference throughout the writing process for a range of purposes:

- to develop the trust needed in a community of writers;
- to be an interested and sympathetic listener;
- to help solve problems and clarify ideas;
- to stimulate ideas;
- to focus on meaning;
- to use partners, groups, and the whole class to model questions that will lead to self-revision;
- to focus on what the learner is learning to use;
- to help the writer with proof-reading and correcting tasks;
- to discuss publication and set deadlines.

Whatever the teacher's goal, the learner's priority must be to acquire strategies to overcome difficulties faced in putting ideas down on paper. The teacher's approach must be to focus on what the writer *can do* rather than *not do*, and lead on from there.

   There are four main conference techniques:

1   Individual—this technique is designed to give feedback to the writer on content, proof-reading, and self-correcting skills, and to discuss publication. Teachers should ensure that the learners focus on **particular** skills and aspects of the process they are trying to develop, not those that are still to come.

Here is an individual conference about capital letters for proper names:

Teacher   Let's have a look here. What do you know about capital letters?

Laura   They're special, and they're used at the beginning of sentences.

Teacher   Yes, and anywhere else? (Referring to the child's skills list) I think we've got this down here. (Reads) "Using capital letters for names", well, let's see. I can see a sort of name and it needs a capital letter. Would you like to look through this and see if you can find it when you do your editing? (Child does so.)

Laura   Mum?

Teacher   Yes, Mum. See here, where your friend Hayley has her name.

Laura   She's got a capital letter.

Teacher   Yes. Mum's not quite like Hayley, but it still needs a capital letter because it's the name you call her. Who would be another person who needs a capital letter?

Laura   Dad?

Teacher   Yes, that's right.

2   Roving—where the teacher moves from writer to writer, making short calls on each one, giving them guidance, and enabling them to make revisions before they have gone too far to make the effort manageable.

3 Group—where groups of writers meet to share their drafts. Learners may choose a conference because they need others to help them solve a problem in their writing ("Where do I go next?"), or because they need to share their writing with a wider audience than a partner.

Conferences actually involve each person in explaining why they are at the conference, and reading part of their writing to the group. The audience listens, bearing in mind the purpose for the writing, and gives supportive feedback.

With training, students almost completely take over the conferencing role, enabling learners to gain responsibility for their own writing, and reducing the degree to which teachers control and shape learners' writing.

Here is an example of a group conference:

Blair, a reluctant eight-year-old, shared his first draft with the class. By asking a series of questions, the class helped Blair clarify his ideas to add information to his writing:

Blair   On Sunday when I was playing rugby, a rugby sprig got up my nose. Mum took me to the hospital. The sprig came out. Mum came to get me to go home.

James   Blair, you said that you got a rugby sprig up your nose. How did it get there?

Blair   Well, I tackled him around his legs—his feet flung up—the sprig went up my nose.

James   Who's him?

Blair   A Bluff boy.

Elizabeth   You said the sprig came out. How did it come out?

Blair   When I was going up the stairs at the hospital, I sneezed into my handkerchief and the sprig came out into my handkerchief. I put my hanky in my pocket.

Tom   Blair, you've told us it came out. How did it feel when it did?

Blair   Relieved.

Peter   What about when it was up your nose? How did it feel then?

Blair   (After a long pause.) Funny—I thought people will laugh at me.

Tony   Blair, you said that your mother took you to hospital and then you said she came to get you. How long did she leave you there?

Blair   Oh, that's wrong. She stayed with me.

Teacher   What are you going to do now, Blair?

Blair   I'm going to rewrite [revise] and add more information.[70]

4   Partner—an introduction to the partner conference could be done with a chart of instructions, for example:

Have your partner tell you about their writing.

Listen to a passage of your partner's writing.

Ask questions about anything you do not understand.

Comment about something in the writing you like. (Give a reason.)

Ask your partner to tell you about today's writing.

Swap over and tell your partner about your writing.

If learners are lacking in self-confidence, allowing them to sit alongside another learner (especially from the same cultural background, and with that person's permission, of course), and watch an individual conference going on, or to share their conference with a partner or friend, often reassures them.[71]

Writers will share willingly with people who understand them and can help them meet their immediate needs. Teachers should be aware that this trust is developed when the class is a community of writers. Groups should be changed to meet the needs of learners.

Teachers must limit the number of issues they ask learners to deal with at any one time. As Donald Murray says:

> *The important thing is that only one or two issues are dealt with in a conference. The conference isn't a psychiatric session. Think of the writer as an apprentice at the workbench with a master workman, a senior colleague, stopping by once in a while for a quick chat about the work.*[72]

Note Murray's implication that most conferences are short and *repeated*. This relates to conferences in all aspects of the writing process—from the very beginning of forming intentions to the outcomes of publishing a text.

The idea of balance

To, with, and by

No one way of teaching children will ensure learning outcomes for them all. However, the balance of approaches which helps them develop successfully as life-long readers is as significant in helping them to become successful writers. This is because learners benefit in different ways from a variety of experiences.

To meet the divergent needs of learners in their classrooms, teachers should plan for a balance of writing approaches, in the same way as they balance their reading approaches. Writing to, writing with, and writing by children provide the contexts in which this balance can be achieved.

Writing/reading to

When they read to children, teachers use models of published texts to demonstrate ways in which writers use appropriate genres, select the words that best express their meaning, shape writing to suit the genre, and structure their writing effectively. This reading provides models which help learners understand how writers communicate thoughts and feelings, information, and ideas.

Teachers need to write *to* children by modelling writing in front of them and talking about the process as they write. In this way, they can establish understandings about the writing process, and demonstrate strategies—from the simplest challenges of forming letters, to the most complex of expressing meaning in a particular genre or style.

Writing/reading with

Shared writing

The shared language, or language experience, approach helps learners at all levels to develop their control of language through an experience which provides the basis for thinking, talking, writing, and reading. The teacher's role in this approach is to help the learner understand that what has been experienced can be talked through, that the talk can be written down, that the writing can be refined, and finally read by others. In this approach, the teacher will very often act as a scribe.

Guided writing

Guided reading enables readers to think, talk, and read their way through a published text by enhancing the strategies through which they interact with the writer's message. Similarly, in guided writing, writers are helped to work through their own text to find the best means of conveying their message to the reader.

The teacher's role in this approach is to provide opportunities for groups of learners to meet and share their writing during the composing stage of the writing process. It is important that the teacher models the sort of questions that help the writer to clarify meaning. The writers should know that the teacher expects them to begin asking similar questions of each other, and eventually of themselves. Learners see writing as the active construction of meaning.

Writing/reading by

Providing time for all learners at all stages of development to read independently is now a well-established practice in most New Zealand classrooms. The practice has risen out of the belief that children learn to read by reading.

Children also learn to write by writing. Classroom organisation must provide time for learners to write every day across all areas of the curriculum. This will enable them to practise what they already know, refine and consolidate what they are learning, and attempt what they are just discovering. Margaret Meek shares this insight into how a child learns to talk:

> *Children's language develops with everyday talk; most of it is directed at getting things done. But there is another kind that emerges when the day's activities are over. You hear it in some children between the ages of two and three, especially if they sleep alone. The child is lying in bed, not expecting attention, and talking to himself. If you listen carefully, you will hear that he is distinguishing sounds and practising them. Then he whispers, shouts, squeaks, sings, and produces a whole range of noises that make up words, like a violinist trying out a new instrument.[73]*

Learner-writers, like learner-talkers, need time to try out the new "instruments" of communication.

Range of genres

It is the teacher's responsibility throughout schooling to introduce learners to a wide range of genres, especially the different forms of expository prose. However, the importance of the narrative genre should not be undervalued. We never lose our love of stories, and we continue to learn a great deal through them about the world.

It is also worth remembering that children will write best in expository genres if they are encouraged to develop their personal observations of the world, rather than simply copying adult models.

Learning through writing across the curriculum

Writing in school should be used in all subjects of the curriculum to increase writing ability. It should cover as many forms and kinds of work as possible and appropriate and be related to the world outside school, initially most especially to the writing that goes on in the learner's home. Family members should be encouraged to help the learner with their writing.

Most children will not grow up to be novelists, poets, or playwrights, but they will need, during their lives, to write notes and instructions, or to write letters to family members, some happy, some of condolence. Some letters may need to explain difficult or sensitive matters. As adults, they may well need to write job applications, or make written contact with lawyers, officials, landlords, government agencies, or business people. They may need to take part in cultural occasions—the speech at the wedding is often given from prepared notes. The practice they have in writing at school should stretch not just across the curriculum but towards the home and world after school.

6

Monitoring Writing

Developing a school writing policy

As children develop as writers, they will come into contact with many different teachers and will have been exposed to many teaching styles. For continuity to be achieved, each school needs to develop a well-thought-out policy on how it is going to best help children become fluent, confident, and independent writers. The needs of children, the teachers' skill and experience, as well as their beliefs about how children learn, will all need to be considered.

In preparing a school policy statement on writing, the staff might ask:

- Can we define what we value in a writer?
- Have we consulted our community members to find out what they value in a writer?
- Is there an informed belief held within the school on how children learn? Is it understood, clearly stated, and available to all staff?
- Does the school and class environment reflect these beliefs and understandings?
- Do all staff have a clear understanding of the writing process and learners' writing development?
- How can we develop writing in all areas of the curriculum?
- How can the school policy reflect the richness of the cultural diversity of the students, and the experiences of both girls and boys?
- How best can we support and help each other in achieving our aims and objectives?
- How shall we monitor our students' progress? What records of their progress shall we keep, and what is the best way of sharing this information with learners, teachers, and parents?

A school policy is successful when the learners are developing as confident writers who see writing as a natural part of their learning. Teachers would also feel confident about their own on-going support and guidance, and the school community would have understanding of, and sympathy with, the school's aims.

In evaluating the outcomes of a school writing policy, the staff may need to examine, in particular, students' attitudes to writing, their understanding of the process, and the quality of the product. This evaluation should not only be concerned with achievements at a given point but should look for trends over time. Schools need to take into account the ways in which they will monitor children's development as writers and this will be stated in their school policy. Continuity in methods of assessment needs to be taken into consideration.

Monitoring individual writing development

To enable teachers to report on individuals, a monitoring system needs to be set up. A monitoring system that is relevant and usable should:

- record useful information accurately, honestly, effectively, and easily;
- provide information about progress;
- provide information for future learning outcomes, both for the individual and group.

A suggested method of monitoring

Teachers will create their own systems of monitoring and recording to suit their school's policy and their individual needs. However, a method is suggested below which involves the use of at least four indicators:

- an exercise book for the teacher's day-to-day observations and comments;
- a recording page in the back of the child's draft writing book;
- a cumulative file of the teacher's observations and examples of the learner's work;
- a child's spelling notebook.

The teacher's day-to-day observations

Each of the teacher's entries is dated and records a significant development in a learner's progress. These developments may be noted as a result of discussions, conferences, or observations, both planned and informal.

> 5.8 _Match Report_ - based on personal experience
> • needed stronger introduction - more background information needed.
> • confused between language used in radio report and newspaper.
> • kept on trying - revising, conferencing, revising until satisfied.
>
> 15·8 Article · (brainstorming) Road Safety - started with a quotation, used resource material well - concise and specific language related to topic.

Teachers can use the criteria outlined in Chapter 3 to monitor the development of their students in the various aspects of the writing process, and also to develop and monitor their own teaching strategies. The criteria can be supported by the ideas in the section on the teacher's role, and by the statements in the table between pages 118 and 120.

Another useful reference is *Keeping School Records,* Book 1, *Primary Progress Records*; and Book 2, *Principles and Practice of Assessment and Evaluation* .[74]

The learner's draft writing book

Entries made in the back of each learner's draft writing book provide a means of both giving feedback to the writer and recording progress made. Behaviours that are identified as potential teaching points are entered in the back of the exercise book adjacent to a column headed, "I am learning to . . ." and will be the focus of the next teaching session with the writer and others with similar needs. Competence in the behaviour allows a dated entry in an accompanying column headed, "I can . . ."

When a book is full, this page can be photocopied and kept in the learner's cumulative file, which will be passed on to the learner's next teacher.

I am learning to	I can ......
use 7/2 ● a capital letter for a name. Jon ———→ 11/2	
11/2 ● a full stop at the end of a sentence ———→ 15/2	
● 19/2 a red pen to edit my writing ——→ 25/2	
25/2 ● a spell-write to check my spelling ——→ 1/3	
6/3 ● a word instead of a numeral when I write. - one instead of 1 two instead of 2 . ——→	10/5 ● commas to give small breaks in my writing. 10/5 ● exclamation marks
12/3 ● take notes, to plan my writing ——→ 14/3	
19/3 ● to read my writing carefully and make sure it makes sense - check the word endings sits, makes etc. come/came ——→	
- 27/3 use a question mark ?-at the end of a question. ——→ 11/4	
● 17/4 y = ies for plural (more than one) try - tries cry - cries ——→ 12/6	
25/4 ● write an article, for the class newspaper ——→ 31/5	
7/6 paragraphs when I focus on something different in my writing ——→ 12/6	
● 20/6 speech marks " " - when someone is talking. "I can sing," said Jon. ——→ 9/7	
● 15/7 write questions for an interview	

115

The cumulative file

The cumulative file may also include a list of words that the learner can spell. Learners can begin keeping this list as soon as they show that they have control of basic, high-frequency words. [75] Those words that the learner knows can be marked with a highlighter pen, a different-coloured highlighter being used each year.

The learner's spelling notebook

Spelling words used in writing can be collected by the learner in a notebook. If this book is kept easily at hand during writing, words can be added to the list. This can be done by the teacher during final correction or during a roving conference. Teachers should be careful not to load some children down with too many words.

All these records can be the basis of teachers' comments to parents and other teachers, and can provide a profile of each learner, showing:

- what the learner can now do;
- what learning experiences are planned;
- how these will be achieved.

Monitoring writing focuses on learners in action. It includes an analysis of their self-correction at all stages of the writing process. Self-correction is probably most significant during drafting and revision, where learners should be encouraged to neatly cross out and rewrite rather than rub out. This enables the writer to check on previous ideas, and the teacher to monitor how and why the writer's ideas and expression have developed. Where learners are encouraged to use a red pen in proof-reading, their self-correction will be evident.

Self-monitoring will be recorded in the comments at the back of the learner's draft writing book and spelling notebook.

When monitoring involves evaluative judgments by others (teachers and other writers), comments should be constructive, supporting the writer's feeling of being an author.

I am pleased to report that since my letter at the end of last term, Johnny has continued to show an obvious enjoyment of books. He is keen to discuss what he has read and is beginning to justify and defend his interpretations.

He is now able to use the library catalogue and knows how to find books related to his needs and interests.

He has developed control over the use of an index and table of contents. He is working on developing his skill in using main and sub headings to more readily locate information related to aspects of the topic he is working on.

... is keen to communicate his thoughts, ideas, feelings and information he has gathered through writing.

His running records indicate that he knows how to help himself when faced with most problems. He is being encouraged to seek help if he cannot overcome a block or the book is too difficult.

Letters to his penfriend show control of form in personal letter writing and his keenness to seek information from outside sources has resulted in a developing control of formal letter writing.

He sees purpose in brainstorming his thoughts and ideas and uses this to organise an intended sequence for draft writing.

He is being encouraged to seek response to his draft as he writes to ensure his intended meaning is intact.

He is becoming more accepting of response from others and his writing now shows increased evidence of revision to clarify meaning.

... s proof reading shows an increased respect for readers. He has maintained control of what he already knows and this term his writing shows that he now has control of quotation marks, commas and apostrophes for possession. He is currently working on the concept of paragraphing.

He displays confidence in using a dictionary to self correct many of his spelling approximations and has control of 75% of the essential words for writing.

This term he has experimented with a variety of styles of writing. His limerick has been published in a class anthology.

Criteria for quality in writing

Individual readers respond to a piece of writing by using their private criteria, basing value judgments on their ability to interact with the author's message and reconstruct a personal meaning. There are as many sets of criteria as there are writing-readers.

When judgments are made by a group, there is a need for a set of criteria that is relevant to the needs of the learners, and which reflects those values in writing that have been agreed between the school and the parent community. Such a set of criteria might be as follows.

THE WRITER IN THE PROCESS	WRITING—THE PRODUCT
1 The message and its effect	
Purpose and meaning	
Does the writer have a purpose for writing and an audience in mind?	Does the writing say something? Does it have meaning? Is the purpose reflected in the form?
Authority	
Can the writer explain the content of the writing?	Does the writing show that the author knows the topic? Is early interest sustained? Is there evidence of observation? Does the writing reflect personal voice? Is the writing honest?
Clarity	
Does the writer feel that the content and vocabulary achieve the intended effect? Does the writer see the benefits of revision?	Is the writing clear and informative? Is there adequate information? Is the information accurate? Is there evidence of revision?

2 Design

Genre and Structure

Did the writer have a plan for how the writing was to be ordered?	Does the writing have structure, order, and coherence, showing: a well-developed sequence of ideas; effective opening, middle, and ending; well-structured paragraphing?
Can the writer identify those characteristics appropriate to the genre used?	Does the writing have appropriate form?

Title

Can the writer explain the choice of title and topic?	Is the title appropriate?

3 Conventions

Spelling

Does the writer approximate the spelling of words that are not known?	Is the spelling accurate, or does the writing show evidence of identifying and/or correction of misspelled words?

Vocabulary

Does the writer feel that he/she can draw on a widening vocabulary?	Is an appropriate vocabulary used, with aptness and economy?
Does the writer consciously select words that are suited to narrative or descriptive writing, or reportage?	Are sentences well linked and varied?

Punctuation

Does the writer feel that he/she is developing more accurate and effective use of punctuation? Can examples of this be identified in the writing?	Is punctuation correct and appropriate?

Handwriting

| Is the writing readable for this stage of the process or development of the learner? | Is the handwriting legible? |

4. Attitude

| Does the writer enjoy writing? | Does the writing show commitment, experimentation with words and ideas, and vitality? |
| Does the writer enjoy sharing their own writing with others and responding to the writing of others? | |

Appendix 1: Some Characteristics of the Writer at Three Broad Overlapping Stages

Learners who are encouraged to practise what they already know have a secure base to work from. They will then be ready to try new ways of working. Their attitudes and understandings will be formed by the pleasure and success they gain from both old and new paths of discovery.

In primary education, these attitudes, understandings, and behaviours can be grouped into three broad overlapping stages: emergent, early, and fluency. As they progress, learners develop and maintain characteristics of each earlier stage. In all stages, there are common elements but different emphases.

The lists in the following table are not checklists into which every child will neatly fit. Human intellectual and social growth is varied and depends upon individual circumstances. **Schools using these lists may need to amend them to suit their own circumstances.** However, the lists will give teachers a general outline of the developing characteristics of learner writers.

The Emergent Writer	The Early Writer	The Fluent Writer
BASIC ATTITUDES TO WRITING	**BASIC ATTITUDES TO WRITING**	**BASIC ATTITUDES TO WRITING**
• is keen to play at writing;	• is keen to write on a variety of topics;	• gains satisfaction from writing in a variety of genres;
• has confidence that personal experience is expressed with meaning in own writing;	• is willing to look for meaning in own writing and seeks help from others to clarify it;	• respects the needs of the reader in relation to topic and purpose of writing;
• is encouraged by own success to write again;	• is confident in own skills and ability to express thoughts quickly and efficiently in writing;	• expects to meet new challenges, but feels confident about them;
• expects writing to be enjoyable;	• expects own writing to be enjoyed by others;	• appreciates the kinds of pleasure different sorts of writing can bring to self and others;
• finds writing rewarding.	• finds attempts to write in a variety of ways rewarding.	• finds writing in different subject areas, in different forms, and for different purposes as rewarding as writing narrative.

(Continued on next page.)

The Emergent Writer	The Early Writer	The Fluent Writer
CONCEPTS ABOUT PRINT • orients a page to start writing; • develops some knowledge of directionality; spaces between words; upper and lower case letters; • is able to make corrections when text is read back by teacher.	**CONCEPTS ABOUT PRINT** • begins to understand the reason for print conventions; starts to use print conventions such as full-stops, capitals, speech marks correctly; • is able to make some corrections to meaning and to surface features.	**CONCEPTS ABOUT PRINT** • uses most print conventions, e.g., italics, colons, semi-colons, line breaks, dashes; • has growing control over surface features; realises that the audience expects to see a correct script—proof-reading is now habitual.
BASIC UNDERSTANDINGS ABOUT WRITING • print holds meaning; • stories can be written down; • speech can be written down; • writing can be read over and over again; • begins to understand that thoughts can be written down; • understands that texts to be shared need further work if they are to reach the audience; • can talk about some features of own writing.	**BASIC UNDERSTANDINGS ABOUT WRITING** • knows that writing has to make sense; • knows words carry many kinds of information; • begins to appreciate the different effects on content when expressed in written rather than oral forms; • begins to realise the importance of writing as a permanent record of events; • begins to understand that writing things down helps clarify meaning; • realises that writing can involve a number of stages; • begins to acquire the "language of the writer".	**BASIC UNDERSTANDINGS ABOUT WRITING** • expects writing to play a major part in daily living and learning; • knows that the written word has special influence and significance in many aspects of social life, e.g., the law, the stage, the media, religion; • refines appreciation of effects on content of expression in written rather than oral forms; • begins to critically assess written records; • sees writing as a tool for learning; • expects to work through the writing process for texts that will be read by others; understands that purpose dictates the use made of writing; • realises the usefulness of the "language of the writer".
TOPIC AND OWNERSHIP • expects own writing to belong to self; • is responsible for own topics and learning; • uses own experience for writing; • is beginning to locate references, e.g., spelling lists; • centres topics largely on own world.	**TOPIC AND OWNERSHIP** • develops own voice; • selects from a wider range of topics; • begins to contextualise own experience in the light of other knowledge; • uses an increasing range of sources to assist writing; • selects topics in different areas of the curriculum.	**TOPIC AND OWNERSHIP** • sees distinctions between objective and subjective writing; • is willing to keep and maintain topic lists; • sees the need for research to discover all the information needed for a topic prior to writing; • has confidence to use study skills that enable location and addition of information; • writes freely on topics in all areas of the curriculum.

The Emergent Writer	The Early Writer	The Fluent Writer
IDEAS AND FORMS • draws pictures and scribbles to generate and express ideas; • explains orally about own pictures; • begins to use simple sentence forms; • links own story title to own story; • is developing an understanding of how books and stories work.	**IDEAS AND FORMS** • draws, discusses, jots, scribbles to fix and structure initial ideas; • talks freely about a topic, using language to develop ideas in brainstorming and discussion; • uses sentence structures confidently; • makes use of appropriate headings; • has an understanding of text forms, e.g., middles, beginnings, and endings in different genres.	**IDEAS AND FORMS** • uses notes and plans to assist expression of ideas; • has repeated discussion in the development of ideas; • uses complex sentence forms and starts to set out writing in paragraphs and sections; • titles and subheads text appropriately; • starts to build plot, characters, setting, purpose, suspense, and climax into narrative; uses a variety of ways to lead in to writing; uses a range of written forms and selects the one most appropriate; begins to appreciate register.
FEEDBACK AND MODELLING • is learning to write by watching the teacher's models and from own knowledge of familiar texts; • expects the teacher to help in developing text; • asks questions about others' stories.	**FEEDBACK AND MODELLING** • innovates on models as well as creating own texts; • expects constructive feedback from the teacher and others; • realises that the questions others ask can help in own writing.	**FEEDBACK AND MODELLING** • continues to make use of a variety of models to assist writing; • expects a critical response from the audience when writing is published; • makes constructive critical comment on others' texts.
REVISING AND DRAFTING • adds on to own story; • reads own story back; • begins to realise writing can be changed or reworked; • starts using a word processor to compose text.	**REVISING AND DRAFTING** • starts to insert information; • reads over own writing to check for meaning; • is willing to improve own writing by making changes; • refines keyboard skills; makes changes on screen.	**REVISING AND DRAFTING** • places relevant information strategically and revises text to accommodate new ideas and information; • understands reasons for revising writing; • sees need to continually ask self questions about own writing; • can use more sophisticated features of a word processor.

(Continued on next page.)

The Emergent Writer	The Early Writer	The Fluent Writer
PRESENTATION AND PUBLISHING • selects text to be "published" and shared with others; • experiments with letter shapes to arrive at consistency of letter form; • uses pictures as a basis for writing; • uses a word processor to create text.	**PRESENTATION AND PUBLISHING** • begins to make decisions about how own text will be published; • begins to form letters accurately and with correct movements; is developing skill and ease in handwriting; • presents text with varied illustrations; • begins to arrange and format text with a word processor.	**PRESENTATION AND PUBLISHING** • experiments with different ways of publishing text; knows that the way a text is illustrated helps the reader; • shows competence and skill in handwriting, using cursive form; • uses a layout book or word processor to format text; • makes wide use of computer skills in presenting text.
SPELLING • is prepared to attempt the spelling of unknown words by taking risks; • begins to realise that words are always spelled the same; • shows some knowledge of alphabet through production of letter forms to represent message; develops sound-letter relationships; • is beginning to use sequencing strategies to make words; • can recognise a few key words; • has control of some essential words; • can correct words with the teacher's help; • uses own and class spelling lists; • uses a spelling checker to assist in the spelling of unknown words.	**SPELLING** • is prepared to attempt the spelling of unknown words by taking risks; • understands that spelling is consistent; • knows alphabet; • knows that sounds have letters that represent them; • know letters are ordered to make words; • is in transition from great reliance on sound to letter relationships to greater reliance on visual representations; • is developing mastery of words used in own writing; • starts to self-correct text; • is becoming familiar with the use of dictionaries; • uses a spelling checker to extend knowledge of the rules of spelling as well as confirming text.	**SPELLING** • is prepared to attempt the spelling of unknown words by taking risks; • meets alternative spellings (American/British) without loss of confidence; • knows alphabet; • uses sound to letter relationships when uncertain of correct spelling; • knows that spelling sequences are largely consistent; • develops spelling based on syllabification, knowledge of pattern etc.; • accumulates large body of known words; has mastery of irregular spellings; • has a "spelling conscience"; • has consolidated dictionary skills and applies these during proof-reading; • uses a spelling checker to make text perfect.

Appendix 2: Special Challenges in Teaching Writing

The very young learner-writer

Many teachers wonder just how to start teaching a child to write. There is no one day on which this happens. Children have been developing an awareness of print and its relation to expressing meaning in all sorts of ways from babyhood. Their understanding of writing has been developing alongside their understanding of reading, and they have been busy drawing, scribbling, and making marks on paper. When children first enter school, they are encouraged to use what they know by drawing a picture and talking and writing about it.

At this time, children begin to understand the concept that ideas and sounds can be written down in symbols. This is an exciting intellectual challenge for them. Cracking the code will fascinate most minds, and may seem to over-ride other considerations for a time. However, it is important to base the young learner's interest in the mechanics of written systems on the meanings that writing conveys. Children whose love of books and stories is firmly based will not lose their interest in the messages which words carry as they try to gain control over written symbols.

Once children have realised that writing is a code, and that it can be understood, they put this knowledge to use in developing their skill in saying things in written as well as spoken form. The emphases of the writing programme change, therefore, as their competence develops. The following conference shows a child coming to grips with the idea that a code of written symbols expresses meaning.

Teacher	What are you writing about today, Todd?
Todd	Jack and Jill.
Teacher	And is this your writing? (Pointing to a row of circles.)
Todd	Yes.
Teacher	Can you read it?
Todd	(Pointing to each circle in perfect one-to-one matching.) Jack and Jill went up the hill to fetch . . .
Teacher	What's wrong?
Todd	(Picking up his pencil.) I haven't finished yet.

Children will be at all stages of development, but, like Todd, they should be encouraged to write for themselves from the first day at school and read what they have written, even when their approximations are not easily recognisable. It is important that their message is then modelled by the teacher either in the form of a published book which the learner can share with an audience, or modelled as correct text underneath.

Teachers should not expect instant results, for the child may take a view of the demonstration entirely different from what the teacher had in mind. Consider:

Principal That's a big story you have there today. Can you read it to me? (Pointing to several rows of letters.)

Susan Last Saturday we went to Riverton. Dad and I had a swim and the water was cold and Mum sat on the beach.

Principal And that's your writing? Whose writing is this? (Pointing to where the teacher had neatly recorded the beach story underneath.)

Susan That's the teacher's. She copied off me.

In the first years, children must acquire enough letter-sound knowledge to be able to approximate spelling so that they can construct text. For most teachers of year one and two children, the daily task of sitting with them and talking through their attempts at spelling new words may seem never ending. However, until children acquire this knowledge, they will not develop as writers. In the first part of their writing career, alphabet knowledge, letter-sound association, and developing a written sight vocabulary must be the major teaching tasks. But if children start out as writers and gain this basic knowledge, they will have the confidence to step out on their own.

Resources which give detailed advice on classroom organisation and teaching strategies for the beginning writer are planned to support this book. (See Introduction, page 8.)

Writing for new learners of English

"There are many similarities between developing writing skill in a first and second language."[76] New learners of English face the same sort of challenges as native speakers but to a greater degree. There are many factors which influence their ability to write a second language, and the time they will take to reach fluency. However, the writing process is basically the same for all.

One of the first things to realise about new learners of English is the great diversity of their educational backgrounds. Some may be extremely knowledgable and able to write in one or more languages, although English is not one of these. It is important not to underestimate their abilities or their intelligence.

For those who do not speak English well, or at all, it is important that they are not overwhelmed with learning too many things at once. Coping with a

126

different orthography, for example, may be the problem for those who can write in their own language but not in English. For others, their first efforts must go to developing spoken English, but alongside this they should have every opportunity to write in their own language. Later, their spoken and written English should be practised side by side, and their reading and writing develop hand in hand. Extensive easy reading is essential in helping learners of a second language reach fluency.

Those who cannot read or write at all need as much practice in scribbling and drawing as any very young child. This first "writing" would need to be done as they work in a bilingual situation, using their own first language to help them in their understanding of spoken English. Once children begin to speak some English, they can begin to write it long before they have complete control over it. One strategy is often termed the "language experience" approach—children learn to write what they themselves have created in speech. This text is used as a basis for exchanging ideas about the content, and discussing print elements and conventions.[77] However, above all, children need to feel secure in their first language and have the opportunity to continue to write in it—to friends and relatives. Only then will they come to feel secure in English. Parents and community members should be involved in developing this self-confidence.

Valuing a child's own culture and background, whatever their level of development or competence in English, is something that will promote their confidence and interest in writing as they progress through the school. Children writing about their experiences need the same kind of response as first-language speakers to *what* they are saying before their words are picked apart in the interests of "correctness". A teacher comments:

> *I've had some marvellous writing from kids, that was totally ungrammatical, unpunctuated, circular, involved, very tortuous, terrible, but there's a real person coming through, expressing something very deep in them.*[78]

Teachers who have children with second language needs in their classes are referred for help to the new settlers and multicultural co-ordinators at colleges of education. (Refer also to the Department of Education handbook, *New Voices*, in the "Finding out more" section below.) The implications for organising in the classroom for these children should be stated as policy in the school charter.

Resources which give detailed advice on classroom organisation and teaching strategies for the new learners of English are planned to support this book. (See Introduction, page 8.)

A Glossary of Important Terms

Edit

This word is often used to signify two stages in making writing correct for the reader—the first use is during the revision stage, when major restructuring, reordering, and clarification of text can take place. At this point, the writer teases out thought, searching for the right words and forms to express meaning.

At a later stage, when the shaping of the writing is satisfactory, minor editing will be used to polish the text, improving expression at the sentence level, correcting surface features of spelling and punctuation, checking facts and references, diagrams, captions, illustrations, and layout.

Exposition/expository prose/transactional prose

These terms describe text which sets out to present or convey an argument, to state the solution to a problem, to explain a situation, or to describe objects or processes in an objective manner. Facts and information rather than perceptions or emotions are the hallmark of exposition, but it is often extremely difficult to ensure that any language used is not loaded with the writer's attitudes or preconceptions.

Form/structure

These terms refer to the construction, organisation, design, and sequence of ideas in a piece of writing which make its meaning and development clear, or make it specific to the genre, for example, iambic pentameter, sonnet, haiku, limerick, or epic. Elements of the structure would include the way the writing begins, the arrangement and sequencing of the material, and the way it finishes.

Genre

Genre refers to the different literary types, classes, sets, or categories of writing, each featuring its own group of attributes—in content, style, and form. Traditionally, genre has applied to groups such as the novel, short story, poetry, science fiction, drama, and so on. It may also be applied to other distinctions such as "personal", "imaginative", or "expository" writing, or to kinds of writing such as diaries, personal letters, business letters, advertisements, lists. The attributes of each genre are conditioned by the *purpose* for the writing and, except in a limited number of genres, are not obligatory—there is no *one* way to write a novel, for example, but there are common expectations of what a novel will contain.

Register

This is a term encompassing language variation dependent on appropriate interaction. Language differs in register according to who the speaker/writer is, the occasion on which they are speaking/writing, what they are speaking/writing about, and who they are speaking/writing to. For example, register involves different language in the law, business, journals, or particular sports. Register is distinguished by a particular vocabulary and often by particular structures. It is necessary to have a range of registers to cope with different social roles, functions, and contexts.

Style

Style represents the particular ways in which things are spoken or written, and by which, through consistent use, unique characteristics of expression can be identified. From a more individual aspect, style may be reflected in the way writing often evokes a feeling in the reader that the author has striven for the most effective way to express personal thoughts and emotions in order to suit a particular purpose. A distinctive style may be emulated by others. When the qualities that characterise an individual's writing are discerned as being similar to those shown by another recognised writer, the characteristics are referred to as a "style", for example, a rhetorical style.

Voice

Voice refers to those aspects of a piece of writing that give it a personal flavour. It is a term coined by Donald Graves. A definition such as "personal style" nearly suffices, but the "voice" also reflects the personal confidence of the writer. It may have less stability and consistency than style, and be relevant to a particular event—"voice" is often modified by the chosen genre, fashions, and the prevailing media. Above all it expresses the writer's confidence of expression.

Finding Out More

NOTE: Not all the books mentioned in this section will still be in print and some may be kept in specialised libraries—librarians will make a search for you on request. The National Library should be able to supply copies of many of the books listed, and often photocopies of articles, or to tell you where requested material is held. However, teachers should realise that, if a good book is not available in New Zealand, libraries are open to suggestions to buy a copy, provided sufficient justification for the request is given. A charge may be made for the administrative costs of a search, and for borrowing or purchasing books. In any case, teachers could keep their eyes on the book review pages of professional journals, and the latest treasures in their local bookshops.

1: Beliefs and Principles (pp.9-20)

If you would like to read some general books on writing and teaching writing, try:

Britton, J. *Language and Learning.* Penguin, Harmondsworth, Middlesex, 1970. Britton has written one of the classic books on language development.

The Best of Set: Writing. New Zealand Council for Educational Research, Wellington, 1992.
This collection includes a range of articles on aspects of learning, teaching, and assessing writing.

Calkins, L. M. *The Art of Teaching Writing.* Heinemann, Portsmouth, New Hampshire, 1986.
Lessons from a Child: on the teaching and learning of writing. Heinemann, Portsmouth, New Hampshire, 1983.
With S. Harwayne. *Living Between the Lines.* Teachers College, Columbia University. Heinemann, Portsmouth, New Hampshire, 1991.
Lucy Calkins's books are full of practical examples of teaching writing. The last book (above) contains her thoughts on the latest developments in her writing projects. She points out (on p. 129) that the writing workshop can be altered to suit other and wider purposes.

Cambourne, B. *The Whole Story: natural learning and the acquisition of literacy in the classroom.* Ashton Scholastic, Auckland, 1988.
Cambourne describes conditions in which children's reading and writing flourish.

Clay, M. M. *Becoming Literate: the construction of inner control.* Heinemann, Auckland, 1991.
This comprehensive book explores in great detail how young children learn to read.

DeStefano, J. for the National Conference on Research in English. "Demonstrations, Engagement and Sensitivity: a revised approach to language learning—Frank Smith." in *Language Arts,* vol. 58, no. 1, 1981.
This is a report of an important address by Smith. It includes the concept of "engagement".

Graves, D. H. *Writing: teachers and children at work.* Heinemann, Exeter, New Hampshire, 1983.
Graves is well known to teachers, and this book is a definitive text on writing. The index will cue teachers in to many answers to their questions.

Hall, N. *The Emergence of Literacy.* Edward Arnold/Hodder and Stoughton, Great Britain, 1987.
Hall offers a compact account of research into emergent literacy, supported by examples of children's talk and actions.

Holdaway, D. *Stability and Change in Literacy Learning.* Heinemann, Portsmouth, New Hampshire, 1985.
The Foundations of Literacy. Ashton Scholastic, Auckland, 1979.
Holdaway is an outstanding New Zealand educator in language and literacy learning.

Murray, D. *Learning by Teaching.* Boynton/Cook, Upper Montclair, New Jersey, 1982.
Write to Learn. Holt, Rinehart and Winston, New York, 1984.
A Writer Teaches Writing: a practical method of teaching composition. Houghton Mifflin, Boston, 1986.
Murray is another of the leading authorities on the teaching of writing.

Smith, F. *Writing and the Writer.* Holt, Rinehart, and Winston, New York, 1981.
"Myths of Writing" in *Language Arts,* vol. 58, no. 7, 1981.
Frank Smith has had considerable influence on New Zealand teachers in both reading and writing. He is well worth reading, and makes some penetrating points about conventional ideas on writing. (See DeStefano, above.)

Wells, G. *The Meaning Makers.* Heinemann, Exeter, New Hampshire, 1986.
This is a good general introduction to basic ideas about writing.

2: The Writing Process (pp.21-5)

If you would like to read some general books on the writing process in schools, try:

Carruthers, A., Philips, D., Rathgen, E., and **Scanlon, P.** *The Word Process.* Longman Paul, Auckland, 1991.

This book, written by and for New Zealanders, is based on the Writing Project in-service model popularised in the United States of America, but adapted to suit New Zealand conditions. It has secondary-level emphases.

Collerson, J. (ed) *Writing for Life.* Primary English Teaching Association, Sydney, 1988.

A useful collection of perspectives from different authors on the writing process. The book ranges across primary and secondary school age levels, and across different genres. It contains a useful bibliography.

See also **Graves** and **Murray** in the previous section.

3: The Writing Process in Action

Forming Intentions: choosing topics (pp.27-34)

If you would like to find out more about topic choice, try:

Dalton, J. *Adventures in Thinking: creative thinking and co-operative talking in small groups.* Thomas Nelson, Melbourne, 1985.

Contained in this valuable book on creative thinking and social interaction is some useful advice on generating topics.

Graves, D. *Writing: teachers and children at work.* Heinemann, Exeter, New Hampshire, 1983.

There are many references to topic choice throughout Graves's book.

Stewart-Dore, N. (ed) *Writing and Reading to Learn.* Primary English Teaching Association, Sydney, 1986.

This account of using writing across the curriculum illustrates the range of topics which this kind of programme generates.

Ward, G. *I've Got a Project.* Primary English Teaching Association, Sydney, 1988.

This is a short, clear, readable book on using a theme to generate writing.

Forming Intentions: determining the audience (pp.34-7)

If you would like to find out more about ways in which writer and audience inter-relate, try:

McVitty, W. *Talking to Writers.* Bookshelf. Martin Educational/Ashton Scholastic, Auckland, 1989.

Well-known authors talk about where they get their ideas and how they write their books.

Mooney, M. *Listen to the Authors. The Highgate Collection.* Nelson Price Milburn, Wellington, 1989.

The teachers' guide to *The Highgate Collection* reading books for middle primary classes contains many comments from authors about their perception of audience and how this affects their work.

Other sources which show how authors themselves see their own audiences may be found in the journals *Children's Literature in Education*, and *The Horn Book Magazine* .

O'Rourke, A. and **Philips, D.** *Responding Effectively to Pupils' Writing.* New Zealand Council for Educational Research, Wellington, 1989.

This report of the study of the practices of over sixty New Zealand primary teachers (considered "effective"), of which twenty-four were closely observed in action, contains many examples of audience response and feedback.

Smith, F. *Writing and the Writer.* Heinemann, London, 1982.

In this excellent text, Smith discusses the writer's perception of audience.

Forming Intentions: finding out, selecting, and ordering information (pp.37-46)

If you would like to find out more about ways of focusing, selecting, and ordering information, or ways of researching topics, try:

Flower, L. *Problem-Solving Strategies for Writing.* Harcourt Brace Jovanovich, New York, 1989. (3rd ed)

This book contains extensive advice, on material at a more advanced level, about the many ways in which topic knowledge can be identified, researched, and planned. The book also has good sections on logical analysis and organisation of text.

Derewianka, B. *Exploring How Texts Work.* Primary English Teaching Association, Sydney, 1990.

Derewianka's short practical book describes how children create different kinds of functional writing. Each chapter has a "summary of text features" related to the kind of text described. Chapter 5: Information Reports gives a stimulating account of children researching how a telephone works, and the language they needed to communicate and record their discoveries.

"Unit 8 Study Skills". LARIC: *Later Reading Inservice Course* , Department of Education, Wellington, 1983.
This unit in the *Later Reading Inservice Course* gives explicit advice on helping older students acquire study skills. It also shows ways of expanding topics into sub-topics, and of producing an organised "semantic web" rather than one built by association of ideas only.

Forming Intentions: appropriate forms (pp.46-54)

If you would like to find out more about different forms or genres, try:

Bennett, J. *The Writing Book.* Ashton Scholastic, New South Wales, 1989.
This is a short, handy book of teaching ideas, with a section on writing in different genres.

Collerson, J. (ed) *Writing for Life.* Primary English Teaching Association, Sydney, 1988.
This book contains practical advice on teaching different genres to young learner-writers (narrative and report writing), and has a section on writing across the curriculum in secondary school. The book also has an extensive bibliography.

Derewianka, B. *Exploring How Texts Work.* Primary English Teaching Association, Sydney, 1990.
Each chapter has a "summary of text features" related to the kind of text described.

Dickinson, D. *Write from the Start: a tool kit for young writers.* Macmillan, Melbourne, 1988.
This is a guide to practical techniques for writing in different genres.

Graves, D. H. *Investigate Nonfiction.* Series: The Reading/Writing Teachers' Companion. Heinemann, Portsmouth, New Hampshire, 1989. (Other books in this series are: *Experiment with Fiction, Discover Your Own Literacy, Build a Literate Classroom,* and *Explore Poetry.*)
Graves gives many examples of how to help children in developing writing skill in different genres.

Ink-slinger: poems about putting words on paper, edited by Morag Styles and Helen Cook. A & C Black, London, 1990.
This little book is full of lively examples of the genre of poetry for children—all about getting words going.

Maori for the Office. Te Taura Whiri i te Reo Maori/Maori Language Commission, Te Whanga-nui-a-Tara/Wellington, 1990.
This booklet contains specific guidance on Maori forms in letter writing.

Martin, J.R. *Factual Writing: exploring and challenging social reality.* Deakin University, Victoria, 1985.
This is a thought-provoking book which analyses so-called "objective" prose.

Stewart-Dore, N. (ed) *Writing and Reading to Learn.* Primary English Teaching Association, Sydney, 1986.
This book contains large sections on the characteristics of genres.

Ward, R. S. and **Cawkwell, G**. "Pupils' Writing Out-of-school: the significance for school programmes", in *English in Aotearoa*, 14, May-June 1991, pp. 29-30.
This article discusses the range of forms which children meet with, raising the question of why out-of-school writing experiences are often wider than those in school.

There is an increasing number of picture books for younger readers on technical subjects or processes which illustrate different text genres—narrative, caption, cartoon speech, exposition. Two humorous examples are from *The Magic School Bus Series: Inside the Human Body* and *At the Waterworks*, written by Joanne Cole and illustrated by Bruce Degan. Scholastic, New York, 1989. More technical and fact-packed but still extremely accessible for young readers are series such as the Usborne books. Teachers can also make use of the many different kinds of article in the *School Journal*. The School Library Service is ready with advice.

Composing and Drafting: getting it down on paper—revising as you go (pp.55-60)
If you would like to know more about composing and drafting, try:

Cassedy, S. *Your Own Words: a beginner's guide to writing.* Doubleday, New York, 1979.
This short book contains many ideas for stimulating children's powers of observation and imagination, and for the crafting of different kinds of writing.

Information Technology in the Writing Process (working title). Ministry of Education, Wellington, 1992.
This outlines the use teachers can make of the word processor in the writing process.

Murray, D. *Learning by Teaching: selected articles on writing and teaching.* Boynton/Cook, Upper Montclair, New Hampshire, 1982.

Write to Learn. Holt Rinehart and Winston, New York, 1984.

A Writer Teaches Writing: a practical method of teaching composition. Houghton Mifflin, Boston, 1968.

Expecting the Unexpected: teaching myself—and others—to read and write. Boynton/Cook Publishers and Heinemann, Exeter, New Hampshire, 1989.

The first two books above are classics on the writing process. In the third, Murray takes the reader through his own writing experiences, making many illuminating points and, in the last, he describes in detail his own struggles to create a good piece of writing. These books are also classics on composing and drafting.

Correcting and Publishing: correcting and proofreading (pp.60-70)

If you would like to find out more about proof-reading skills, try:

Dickinson, D. *Write from the Start: a tool kit for young writers.* Macmillan, Melbourne, 1988.

This book contains sections on the surface features of writing.

Gentry, R. *Spel is a Four Letter Word.* Ashton Scholastic, Auckland, 1987.

Gentry's book describes the acquisition of correct spelling and how to help a struggling speller achieve success.

Graves, D. *Writing: teachers and children at work.* Heinemann, Exeter, New Hampshire, 1983.

Graves makes some important teaching points about the roles of the learner and the teacher in correcting text.

Guidelines for Authors: preparing manuscripts for publication, edited by Paula Wagemaker. New Zealand Government Printing Office, Wellington, 1984.

This manual is a clear, technical description of the preparation of texts for publication.

Correcting and Publishing: publishing (pp.70-9)

If you would like to find out more about publishing, try:

Information Technology in the Writing Process (working title). Ministry of Education, Wellington, 1992.

This outlines the use teachers can make of the word processor in the writing process.

Morris, N. *The Lettering Book.* Ashton Scholastic, New South Wales, 1981.

The Lettering Book Companion. Ashton Scholastic, New South Wales, 1987.

Both of these books are written for young (8 to 12-year-old) writers and contain simple instructions, with many examples of lettering and decorative design.

The School Journal, special seventy-fifth jubilee issue, School Publications Branch, Department of Education, Wellington, 1982.
This issue describes the process of how a book is made. It is a useful example of the steps in the publication process.

Teaching Handwriting: supplement to the syllabus Language in the Primary School: English. Department of Education, Wellington, 1985.

And if you would like to read more about the influence of medium on message, try:

Postman, N. *Amusing Ourselves to Death: public discourse in the age of show business.* Heinemann, London, 1986.
This is a provocative book about written language, the visual media, and what they do to the way we think.

Outcomes: audience response (pp.79-84)
If you would like to find out more about audience response, try:

Dalton, J. *Adventures in Thinking: creative thinking and co-operative talking in small groups.* Thomas Nelson, Melbourne, 1985.
This contains guidance on how to run a constructive discussion.

Lamb, H. F. *Writing Performance in New Zealand Schools: a report on the IEA study of written composition in New Zealand.* Department of Education, Wellington, 1987.
Hilary Lamb records varied kinds of teacher feedback and comments on their effectiveness.

Mc Naughton, S. and Ka'ai, T. *Two Studies of Transition: Socialization of Literacy* and *Te Hiringa Take Take: mai i te kōhanga reo ki te kura.* Maori Research and Development Unit, Department of Education, University of Auckland, Auckland, 1990.
See the earlier comments relating to conferences (page 53) on the importance of social and cultural influences in responding effectively to learners' writing.

O'Rourke, A. and **Philips, D.** *Responding Effectively to Pupils' Writing.* New Zealand Council for Educational Research, Wellington, 1989.
The report contains much information on teachers' responses and feedback.

4: Young People's Writing (pp.85-98)

Cassedy, S. *Your Own Words: a beginner's guide to writing.* Doubleday, New York, 1979.

This book gives some excellent advice on how to encourage quality in children's writing. It is not widely held in New Zealand, but worth the effort to obtain and read.

5: Organising for Writing (pp.99-111)

If you would like to find out more about organising for writing, try:

Dalton, J. *Adventures in Thinking: creative thinking and co-operative talking in small groups.* Thomas Nelson, Melbourne, 1985.

This book has many thoughts and ideas on grouping according to the needs of learners and teachers, and ways into creative talk on a variety of topics.

Graves, D. *Writing: teachers and children at work.* Heinemann, Exeter, New Hampshire, 1983.

Graves's classic book gives advice on organisation, especially on establishing a workshop.

Hill, S. and **Edwards, F.** *Language and Learning in Secondary Schools: Science.* Learning Media, Ministry of Education, Wellington, 1992.

Language and Learning in Secondary Schools: Mathematics. Learning Media, Ministry of Education, Wellington, 1991.

Both the above books are written for the junior secondary school, but contain many practical ideas on classroom management which help students come to grips with the language of the curriculum.

Heenan, J. *Writing: process and product: a guide to class and school programmes.* Longman Paul, Auckland, 1985.

This New Zealand educator's account of his experiences in teaching writing offers close-to-home examples of organising workshops in writing.

McNaughton, S. and **Ka'ai, T.** *Two Studies of Transition: Socialization of Literacy* and *Te Hiringa Take Take: mai i te kōhanga reo ki te kura.* Maori Research and Development Unit, Department of Education, University of Auckland, Auckland, 1990.

McNaughton's research report into the importance of social and cultural influences in the early literacy of high-progress readers, and Ka'ai's research into literacy characteristics and strategies of kōhanga reo children both deal with interpersonal relationships which have a bearing on how to respond effectively to learners' writing.

Martin, N., D'Arcy, P., Newton, B., and **Parker, R.** *Writing and Learning Across the Curriculum.* Ward Lock , London, 1976.

This is a readable and wide-ranging book of case studies and interpretations of findings, based on research in English schools.

O'Rourke, A. and **Philips, D.** *Responding Effectively to Pupils' Writing.* New Zealand Council for Educational Research, Wellington, 1989.

This report of the study of the practices of over sixty New Zealand primary teachers (considered to be "effective"), of which twenty-four were closely observed in action, contains extended accounts of classroom management ranging from junior primary to intermediate levels, and a discussion on writing in Forms 4 and 6. The book contains sections on organisation at the various levels, and on teaching learners whose first language is not English.

Ward, R. S. "Group Conferencing in Written Language with Older Children" in *New Zealand Principal,* vol. 1, no. 3, 1989, p. 30.

"Discussion: coping with conventions" in *English in Aotearoa,* no. 3, July 1987, pp. 48-9.

Both articles give practical advice about running successful conferences.

6: Monitoring Writing (pp.112-20)

If you would like to find out more about monitoring, assessing, recording, or evaluating learners' writing, try:

Daly, E. (ed) *Monitoring Children's Language Development.* Australian Reading Association, Melbourne, 1990.

This comprehensive book offers teachers many ideas on monitoring.

Keeping School Records: principles and practice of assessment and evaluation and *Primary Progress Records.* Department of Education, Wellington, 1989.

The detailed criteria for language and other curriculum areas offer practical guides for teaching goals.

McPherson, J. and **Corson, D.** *Language Policy Across the Curriculum: eight case studies of school-based policy development.* Department of Education, Massey University, Palmerston North, 1989.

These case studies will suggest avenues of experiment.

If you would like to find out more about the young learner-writer, try:

Bissex, G. *GNYS AT WRK: a child learns to write and read.* Harvard University Press, Cambridge, Massachusetts, 1980.
This is a record of the author's own child's development as a reader and a writer.

Clay, M. M. *What Did I Write?* Heinemann, Auckland, 1975.
Marie Clay takes an in-depth look at the very early stages of writing.
Writing Begins at Home: preparing children for writing before they go to school. Heinemann, Auckland, 1987.
Clay offers good advice for parents and caregivers about the child's introduction to literacy.

Meek, M. *Learning to Read.* The Bodley Head, London, 1982.
This is a perceptive account for teachers and parents of how a young child learns to talk and read.

See also, **Heenan**, **Graves**, **Calkin**, and **Holdaway**.

If you want to find out more about teaching new learners of English, try:

Hill, S. and **Edwards, F.** *Language and Learning in Secondary Schools: Science.* Learning Media, Ministry of Education, Wellington, 1992.
This book contains some useful advice on preparing material for ESL learners.

Holmes, J. *Language for Learning: education in the multicultural school.* Department of Education, Wellington, 1982.
Holmes offers a general introduction on the nature of linguistic diversity, the cultural and linguistic factors involved in learning language, and the importance of teachers', parents', and pupils' attitudes.

Littlewood, W. *Communicative Language Teaching: an introduction.* Cambridge University Press, Cambridge, 1981.
This is a lucid, concise, and practical book containing many examples of language teaching activities and practice.
Foreign and Second Language Learning: language acquisition research and its implications for the classroom. Cambridge University Press, Cambridge, 1984.
This is a clear and useful account of theory and practice.

New Settlers and Multicultural Education Issues. Learning Media, Ministry of Education, Wellington. The last issue of this journal was vol. 7, no. 3, November 1990. It has been replaced by a new journal, *Many Voices*, whose first issue is no. 1, November 1991.

The new journal has been more closely tied to the needs of educators. Interested readers should inquire at Learning Media, Box 3292, Wellington, about availability. Copies of articles in these journals can be obtained through School Library Service.

New Voices: second language learning and teaching: a handbook for primary teachers. Department of Education, Wellington, 1988.

Teachers are particularly referred to the chapters on first language maintenance and literacy in the classroom. The book contains a comprehensive bibliography.

Select Bibliography

The following works have been selected as offering a good basis for teachers' professional reading.

Bissex, G. *GNYS AT WRK; a child learns to write and read.* Harvard University Press, Cambridge, Massachusetts, 1980.

Calkins, L. M. *The Art of Teaching Writing.* Heinemann, Portsmouth, New Hampshire, 1986.

Lessons from a Child. Heinemann, Portsmouth, New Hampshire, 1983.

Cambourne, B. *The Whole Story.* Ashton Scholastic, Auckland, 1988.

Clay, M. M. *What Did I Write?* Heinemann, Auckland, 1973.

Writing Begins at Home: preparing children for writing before they go to school. Heinemann, Auckland, 1987.

Becoming Literate: the construction of inner control. Heinemann, Auckland, 1991.

Dalton, J. *Adventures in Thinking: creative thinking and co-operative talking in small groups.* Thomas Nelson, Melbourne, 1985.

Gentry, J. R. *Spel is a Four Letter Word.* Ashton Scholastic, Auckland, 1987.

"An Analysis of Developmental Spelling in *GNYS AT WRK*" in *The Reading Teacher,* November 1982, pp. 192-9.

Graves, D. H. *Investigate Nonfiction.* Heinemann, Portsmouth, New Hampshire, 1989. (Other books in *The Reading/Writing Teachers' Companion* series are: *Experiment with Fiction, Discover Your Own Literacy, Build a Literate Classroom,* and *Explore Poetry.*)

Writing: teachers and children at work. Heinemann, Exeter, New Hampshire, 1983.

Heenan, J. *Writing: process and product: a guide to class and school programmes.* Longman Paul, Auckland, 1985.

Hill, S. and **Edwards, F.** *Language and Learning in Secondary Schools: Science.* Learning Media, Ministry of Education. Wellington, 1991.

Holdaway, D. *Stability and Change in Literacy Learning.* Heinemann, Exeter, New Hampshire, 1984.

The Foundations of Literacy. Ashton Scholastic, Sydney, 1979.

Lamb, H. F. "Learning and Teaching Writing" (IEA Written Composition Study) in *SET* no. 1 1989. New Zealand Council for Educational Research, Wellington, 1989.

Writing Performance in New Zealand Schools: a report on the IEA study of written composition in New Zealand. Department of Education, Wellington, 1987.

Murray, D. M. *A Writer Teaches Writing: a practical method of teaching composition.* Houghton Mifflin, Boston, 1968.

Learning by Teaching: selected articles on writing and teaching. Boynton/Cook, Upper Montclair, New Jersey, 1982.

Write to Learn. Holt Rinehart and Winston, New York, 1984.

Expecting the Unexpected: teaching myself—and others—to read and write. Boynton/Cook Publishers and Heinemann, Exeter, New Hampshire, 1989.

O'Rourke, A. and **Philips, D.** *Responding Effectively to Pupils' Writing.* New Zealand Council for Educational Research, Wellington, 1989.

Richardson, E. *In the Early World.* New Zealand Council for Educational Research, Wellington, 1964.

Smith, F. *Writing and the Writer.* Heinemann, Auckland, 1982.

Endnotes

1. See chapter 4 on quality in children's writing, and pages 118-20 on criteria for value judgments.
2. Clay, M.M. *What Did I Write?* Heinemann, Auckland, 1973, p. 70.
3. Byatt, A. S. *Sugar and Other Stories.* Chatto and Windus, London, 1987, p. 245.
4. Wells, G. *The Meaning Makers.* Heinemann, Exeter, New Hampshire, 1986, p. 111.
5. Holdaway, D. *Stability and Change in Literacy Learning.* Heinemann, Exeter, New Hampshire, 1984, p. 3.
6. Tizard, B. and Hughes, M. *Young Children Learning: talking and thinking at home and at school.* Fontana, London, 1984. Barbara Tizard and Martin Hughes illustrate some differences in the ways children's talk with adults at home and at school enhances their learning and understanding.
7. See McNaughton, S. and Ka'ai, T. for a discussion about the socialisation of literacy in *Two Studies of Transition: Socialization of Literacy* and *Te Hiringa Take Take: mai i te kōhanga reo ki te kura.* Maori Research and Development Unit, Department of Education, University of Auckland, Auckland, 1990.
8. Grace, P. *Ruia Taitea.* New Zealand Film Commission/Nautilus television programme. Learning Media item number 90/106.
9. McNaughton and Ka'ai, op. cit., p. 55.
10. Grace, P. *Ruia Taitea,* op. cit.
11. Grace, P. *Ruia Taitea,* ibid.
12. Calkins, L. M. *The Art of Teaching Writing.* Heinemann, Exeter, New Hampshire, 1983, p. 10.
13. Cassedy, S. *In Your Own Words: a beginner's guide to writing.* Doubleday, New York, 1979, p. 115.
14. Cambourne, B. *The Whole Story.* Ashton Scholastic, Auckland, 1988, p. 50.
15. DeStefano, J. S. for the National Conference on Research in English. "Demonstrations, Engagement and Sensitivity: a revised approach to language learning—Frank Smith" in *Language Arts,* vol. 58, no.1, 1981.
16. Cambourne , B. op. cit., 1981, p. 34, and p. 50 ff.
17. Cambourne , B. "Rediscovering natural literacy learning". Unpublished paper, 1986. Quoted in *Pathways of Language Development.* Department of Education and the Arts (Tasmania), ACER, Victoria, 1990.
18. Murray, D. *Learning by Teaching: selected articles on writing and teaching.* Boynton/Cook, Upper Montclair, New Jersey, 1982, p. 10.
19. During this and other stages in the writing process, teachers will need to consider organising for writing in the classroom; see chapter 5.
20. Publishing a work means preparing it to a standard at which it can be read and understood by others—it is now "public", no longer a private communication. Publication can involve formatting the text and diagrams, but some manuscripts are not taken to this stage although they are read by others.
21. Norris, L. "The Thin Pen", in *Ink-slinger: poems about putting words on paper,* edited by Morag Styles and Helen Cook. A & C Black , London, 1990.
22. Grace, P. *Ruia Taitea.* op. cit.
23. Britton, J. *Language and Learning.* Penguin, Harmondsworth, Middlesex, 1970, p. 164.
24. Tizard and Hughes, op. cit.
25. Lamb, H. F. *Writing Performance in New Zealand Schools: a report on the IEA study of written composition in New Zealand.* Department of Education, Wellington, 1987, p. 172.
26. Van Doren, M. (quoting Emerson) in *Liberal Education.* Henry Holt, New York, 1943/4, p.95.
27. Lamb, op. cit., p. 157 ff.

28 See glossary, p. 128, for a definition of the term "genre".

29 Goldby, G. "Science as a Process: a change in emphasis" in *Writing in Science: papers from a seminar with science teachers*. Schools Council Publications, Ward Lock, Glasgow, 1976.

30 O'Rourke, A. and Philips, D. *Responding Effectively to Pupils' Writing*. New Zealand Council for Educational Research, Wellington, 1989, p. 197.

31 Lauris Edmond, in conversation with students for the New Zealand Book Council's Writers-in-Schools Scheme, 1990.

32 Wells, op. cit., p. 202.

33 Graves, D. H. *Writing: teachers and children at work*. Heinemann, Exeter, New Hampshire, 1983, p. 146.

34 Gentry, J. R. "An analysis of developmental spelling in *GNYS AT WRK*" in *The Reading Teacher*, Nov. 1982, pp. 192-9.

35 Croft, C. et al. *Teachers' Manual for Spell-Write*. New Zealand Council for Educational Research, Wellington, 1983, pp. 9-10.

36 *Teaching Handwriting: supplement to the syllabus, Language in the Primary School: English*. Department of Education, Wellington, 1985.

37 Bruner, J. *Actual Minds, Possible Worlds*. Harvard University Press, Cambridge, Massachusetts, 1986, p. 77.

38 From "The Accident", by Simon Connell, John McGlashen College, *Journal of Young People's Writing 3, The Terrible Half-pipe*. Learning Media, Ministry of Education, Wellington, 1992.

39 From "Holiday in the Sounds", by David Thomas, Merrilands School, in *Some Place Wonderful. School Journal* , Part 3 No. 1, School Publications Branch, Department of Education, Wellington, 1988.

40 From an unpublished submission to the *Journal of Young People's Writing*.

41 See Bonallack, J., "To New Zealand with the Early European Settlers", in *Education* magazine, vol. 30, no. 4, pp. 40-6, Department of Education, Wellington, 1981.

42 See "A Play from a Story"—the instructions accompanying "My First Pay Packet" in the *School Journal*, Part 4, No. 3, Learning Media, Ministry of Education, Wellington, 1990.

43-47 From unpublished submissions for the *Journal of Young People's Writing*.

48 From "We Left Home", by Hung in *School Journal*, Part 3, No. 2. School Publications Branch, Department of Education, Wellington, 1985.

49 From "Hurricane Iwa", by Melissa Bowen in *School Journal*, Part 3, No. 2, School Publications Branch, Department of Education, Wellington, 1984.

50 From "Friday of No Mercy", quoting Sarah Watt in *School Journal*, Part 3, No. 1, School Publications Branch, Department of Education, Wellington, 1986.

51 Poem by Chez Leggatt, Taipa Area School, in *Some Place Wonderful*.

52 Poem by Callie Winterburn, quoted in "Nga Kaituhi Toro Kura: Writers in Schools" by Patricia Glensor in *English in Aotearoa*. New Zealand Association for the Teaching of English, Wellington, November, 1990.

53-60 From unpublished submissions to the *Journal of Young People's Writing*.

61 From "Species in Danger" in *School Journal*, Part 3, No. 2, Learning Media, Ministry of Education, Wellington, 1990.

62 From "Tangi" by Joseph Harris, Avondale Intermediate School, in *Some Place Wonderful*.

63-64 From unpublished submissions to the *Journal of Young People's Writing*.

65 A poem by Rosanna Carlyle (Hitchcock), Lincoln Heights School, written on 25 January, 1984. The title poem from *Some Place Wonderful*.

66-67 Unpublished submissions to the *Journal of Young People's Writing*.

68 Rosanna Carlyle (Hitchcock), Lincoln Heights School.

69 O'Rourke and Philips, *Responding Effectively to Pupils' Writing*. New Zealand Council for Educational Research, Wellington, 1989, p. 105.

[70] Heenan, J. *Writing: process and product: a guide to class and school programmes.* Longman Paul, Auckland, 1986, p. 53.

[71] O'Rourke and Philips, op. cit., p. 39.

[72] Murray, D. *Learning by Teaching: selected articles on writing and teaching.* Boynton/Cook, Upper Montclair, New Jersey, 1982, pp. 170-1.

[73] Meek, M. *Learning to Read.* The Bodley Head, London, 1982, p. 33.

[74] *Keeping School Records,* Book 1, *Primary Progress Records;* Book 2, *Principles and Practice of Assessment and Evaluation.* Department of Education, Wellington, 1989.

[75] Croft, op. cit., pp. 13-14.

[76] *New Voices: second language learning and teaching: a handbook for primary teachers.* Department of Education, Wellington, 1988, p. 32.

[77] See the discussion on language experience in *Reading in Junior Classes.* Department of Education, Wellington, 1985, pp. 61-9.

[78] O'Rourke and Philips. op. cit., p. 180.

Index

About the authors:
Ro Griffiths is a Senior Policy Analyst in the Learning and Assessment Section of the Policy Division of the Ministry of Education. He began the development of this book in 1987, when he was an Education Officer in the Curriculum Development Division of the Department of Education, and has seen the project through to completion.

Jan Duncan is District Adviser Reading/Language, Wellington College of Education. She has a keen interest in literacy learning and teaching, and is involved in teacher development both in New Zealand and the United States of America.

Richard Ward is a Senior Lecturer in Language/Reading Education at the School of Education, University of Waikato, where he is also Co-ordinator of the Centre for Literacy Education and Research. He has written articles about children's writing, which is the focus of his research interests.

Harry Hood has been Adviser Junior Classes in Southland since 1980. During this time, he has been involved in promoting teachers' understanding of the writing process in various ways, including leading a national training course for resource teachers, working in in-service courses and at conferences, and writing resource materials.

Sheena Hervey is a Senior Lecturer at the Dunedin College of Education where she is Head of English. She has been interested in the development of children's writing since the early 1980s and has led many courses aimed at helping teachers understand a process approach.

John Bonallack is a former primary school teacher, and is now the Editor of the Parts 3 and 4 *School Journal* and the *Journal of Young People's Writing*.

About the editor:
At the time of writing, Bea Hamer was a general editor in Learning Media. Her background is in teaching English as a first and second language, at school and university.

Acknowledgments

Learning Media wishes to thank the many teachers who have been involved in trialling sections of the material in this book, and those schools, teachers, and pupils whose photographs and examples of work illustrate the ideas presented in it.

Photographs, unless otherwise stated, are by ALAN DOAK.
Those on pages 6 and 8 are by JAMIE LEAN; on pages 7, 10, 13, 25, and 33 by KAREN ANGUS; on page 57, bottom right, by PAUL GAY; on pages 87 and 88 by JOHN BONALLACK.

The illustration on page 57 is by PHILLIP PAEA; on page 78 (Postal Impressions) by NEIL PARDINGTON; on page 86 by BOB KERR; on page 90 by JOHN GILLESPIE; on pages 100 -101 by MARGARET NIEUWLAND.

PATRICIA GRACE's short story, "Butterflies" (on page 15) from her collection *Electric City*, 1987, is reprinted by permission of Penguin Books.